Little Laureates

Northern England Poets

Edited by Angela Fairbrace

Young Writers
First published in Great Britain in 2007 by:
Young Writers
Remus House
Coltsfoot Drive
Peterborough
PE2 9JX
Telephone: 01733 890066
Website: www.youngwriters.co.uk

SB ISBN 978-1 84431 282 5

Foreword

Young Writers was established in 1991 and has been passionately devoted to the promotion of reading and writing in children and young adults ever since. The quest continues today. Young Writers remains as committed to the nurturing of poetic and literary talent as ever.

This year's Young Writers competition has proven as vibrant and dynamic as ever and we are delighted to present a showcase of the best poetry from across the UK and in some cases overseas. Each poem has been selected from a wealth of *Little Laureates* entries before ultimately being published in this, our sixteenth primary school poetry series.

Once again, we have been supremely impressed by the overall quality of the entries we have received. The imagination, energy and creativity which has gone into each young writer's entry made choosing the poems a challenging and often difficult but ultimately hugely rewarding task - the general high standard of the work submitted ensured this opportunity to bring their poetry to a larger appreciative audience.

We sincerely hope you are pleased with this final collection and that you will enjoy *Little Laureates Northern England Poets* for many years to come.

Contents

The Poems

A Journey On Mother Sea

Upon the morn that we left,
The sea so calm, it was;
For on the day that we left,
The world rejoiced, oh yes.
For three months the journey would last,
A journey on Mother Sea.

Another morn we had,
A beauteous morn indeed,
But a storm approach it did,
And Hell did it cause for we did toss and turn,
On that forsaken journey,
The journey on Mother Sea.

A wreck that we are now,
After that foulest of days.
The only hope we have now
Is for an explorer journeying,
Journeying on Mother Sea.

Nicholas Gleavy (11)

This Is Fun . . .

Fun is like the colourful green grass.
Fun looks like people playing fast.

Fun sounds like laughing in the air.
Fun smells like fresh pear.

Fun feels soft.
Fun tastes like running beans.

Fun reminds you of spending time with your family.

Tyler Rawlinson (10)
Belle Vale Primary School, Belle Vale

What Is Fear?

It's black, dark blue and bloody red.
What is it? Fear!
It looks like someone has been murdered.
What is It? Fear!
Worst of all it sounds like a girl screaming.
What is it? Fear!
Fear smells like someone has left the cooker on!
What is it? Fear!
Fear feels like when you turn the tap on and blood comes out!
What is it? Fear!
It tastes like raw tree trunks.
What is it? Fear!
Fear reminds me of people killing innocent people.

Shona Wayland (10)
Belle Vale Primary School, Belle Vale

Anger Is . . .

Anger is the colour of burning red lava.
Anger smells like old rotten eggs.
Anger looks like an exploding volcano.
Anger sounds like a big base drum.
Anger feels like electricity running through my veins.
Anger reminds me of losing my toys.

Connor Goulding (11)
Belle Vale Primary School, Belle Vale

All About Fear

Fear is black like a dark cave in the middle of nowhere,
Fear looks like someone being bullied,
Fear feels like sandpaper,
Fear sounds like a person locked up, crying for help,
Fear reminds me of being unable to move because I am too ill!

Hayley McKinney (11)
Belle Vale Primary School, Belle Vale

Sadness Is . . .

Sadness is blue like the ocean waves,
Sadness feels like being betrayed,
Sadness sounds like my heart has stopped beating,
Sadness smells like the sun overheating,
Sadness looks like a person all alone,
Sadness tastes like a cold stone,
Sadness reminds me of never being
Saved . . . !

Katherine Wareing (11)
Belle Vale Primary School, Belle Vale

Anger In The Darkness

Anger is red like a red-hot chilli pepper.
Anger sounds like a volcano exploding.
Anger tastes like a burning fireball.
Anger smells like an old saggy man's armpits.
Anger looks like a dying man.
Anger feels like rotten eggs.
Anger reminds me of someone being bullied.

Elliot Godber (11)
Belle Vale Primary School, Belle Vale

What Is Anger?

Anger is red like blood and a volcano.
Anger feels like a big rocket exploding.
Anger smells like a slimy sock.
Anger sounds like my mum shouting.
Anger tastes like hot chilli peppers.
Anger reminds me of when I don't get my own way.
Anger looks like red blood!

Kelsey Baxter (11)
Belle Vale Primary School, Belle Vale

What Is Misery?

Misery is dull like a dark, frightening grey.
Misery sounds like thunder and lightning.
Misery tastes like rain.
Misery smells like a drain.
Misery looks like a dark cloud.
Misery feels like a wet dog.
Misery reminds me of a baby screaming.

Courtney Caddick (11)
Belle Vale Primary School, Belle Vale

What Anger Is . . .

Anger is as red as boiling lava.
Anger sounds like a lion growing.
Anger tastes like a red-hot pepper.
Anger smells like a rotten, old, dusty bin.
Anger looks like a steaming hot kettle.
Anger feels like a mouldy, revolting egg.
Anger is so bad it reminds me of my mum screaming!

Bradley Evans-Foster (11)
Belle Vale Primary School, Belle Vale

Cheerful Is . . .

Cheerful is pink like a flower.
Cheerful sounds like someone having a drink.
Cheerful tastes like a bar of chocolate.
Cheerful smells like J-Lo perfume.
Cheerful looks like a bright sun.
Cheerful feels like Majorca's hot sand.
Cheerful reminds me of a good band playing!

Aimee Estlin (11)
Belle Vale Primary School, Belle Vale

Happiness

Happiness is as blue as the midday sky.
Happiness has the sound of the waves at the seaside.
Happiness has the taste of a sweet lollipop.
Happiness reminds me of a lovely summer's day.
Happiness smells of a sweet summer rose.
Happiness is someone playing with their mates.
Happiness is as smooth as a cloud in the sky.

Luke Mulvaney (11)
Belle Vale Primary School, Belle Vale

Sadness Revealed

Sadness is blue like a tear in your eye.
Sadness feels like a child about to cry.
Sadness feels like a cold wave washing over itself.
Sadness smells like people who have died due to bad health.
Sadness sounds like someone moaning in despair near the south.
Sadness tastes dry and crooked in your mouth.
It reminds me of war when people never come home.

Grace Zdesenko (11)
Belle Vale Primary School, Belle Vale

What Is Fear . . . ?

Fear is black like a room closed up.
Fear feels like grass that's dying.
Fear sounds like children crying.
Fear reminds me of roses that have died.
Fear looks like a hundred dead flies.
Fear tastes like mouldy air.
Fear smells like a person who doesn't care!

Jessica Furmedge (11)
Belle Vale Primary School, Belle Vale

Sorrow Is . . .

Sorrow is the colour of the bottom of the sea,
Sorrow looks like the opposite of me,
Sorrow reminds me of a cold winter's night,
Sorrow feels like a bird without flight,
Sorrow smells like rust on an old door,
Sorrow tastes like mouldy cheese on the floor,
Sorrow sounds like screams inside,

What do you think sorrow is?

Lauren Ashworth (11)
Belle Vale Primary School, Belle Vale

Sweetness Is Like . . .

Sweetness is like sugar
Sweetness is as bright as pink
Sweetness smells like an apple pie cooking in an oven
Sweetness reminds me of the day my sister was born
It sounds like nature
Sweetness looks like children playing nicely
Sweetness feels like a heart.

Taylor Wearing (11)
Belle Vale Primary School, Belle Vale

Red-Hot Anger

Anger is the darkest red,
Anger sounds like an erupting volcano,
Anger tastes like chilli pepper,
Anger smells like thick black smoke,
Anger looks like a house burning down,
Anger feels like a thousand nails going into my body,
Anger reminds me of my mum grounding me.

Adam Woodhall (11)
Belle Vale Primary School, Belle Vale

Hunger!

Hunger is like a chocolate-brown sauce with a cherry on top.
Hunger looks like melted white chocolate and brown melted icing.
Hunger smells like a big fat beefburger with huge amounts of
tomato sauce.
Hunger feels like a starving pig.
Hunger tastes like any food you like; just like a gateau cake delight.
Hunger sounds like an elephant's beating heart.
Hunger reminds me of when I starved myself for three days.

Jake Martin (11)
Belle Vale Primary School, Belle Vale

Love

Love is the colour red like lips and lipstick
Love is the colour red and red looks like blood
Love is red and red feels like a bumpy cut
Love is red and berries are red so it tastes like berries
Love is red for hearts so red can be blood and blood smells
like nothing
Love is red and red reminds you of roses.

Ellie Smith (9)
Belle Vale Primary School, Belle Vale

Happiness

Happiness is red like flowers
Happiness sounds like the wind passing by me
It tastes minty and fresh
It smells like a rose closing up
It looks like sparkles flashing in the sky
It feels soft and silky
It reminds me of when I had lots of friends.

Holly Furmedge (8)
Belle Vale Primary School, Belle Vale

Anger

Anger is red like the Devil.
It sounds like I am getting zapped.
It tastes like the Devil is trying to kill me.
It smells of air.
It looks vicious on the face.
It feels like I am dying.
It reminds me of war.

Aaron Thompson (9)
Belle Vale Primary School, Belle Vale

Anger

Anger is red like fire
It looks like something is burning
It reminds me of my dad smacking me when I am naughty
It tastes like burnt chicken
It smells like Hell's fire
It sounds like people screaming.

Ben Andrew Cox (9)
Belle Vale Primary School, Belle Vale

Darkness

Darkness is like the night.
Darkness tastes like burnt ash.
Darkness sounds scary.
Darkness smells like burnt toast.
Darkness looks like pitch-black.

Jade Renshaw
Belle Vale Primary School, Belle Vale

Love

What colour is it? Red.
It sounds loud.
Tastes like sweat.
It smells like blood.
Looks like a heart.
Feels squishy.
It reminds me of love.

Michael Hidderley (8)
Belle Vale Primary School, Belle Vale

Love

Love is red like hearts
Love sounds happy
Love tastes sweet
Love smells nice
Love looks like a heart
Love feels wonderful
Love reminds me of someone I love.

Brandon Rakeeb (8)
Belle Vale Primary School, Belle Vale

Sadness

Sadness sounds like an upset person.
Sadness tastes like salty water.
Sadness smells like a burger.
Sadness looks like they're hurt.
Sadness feels like something is banging.
Sadness reminds you of the sad times you have been through.

Jamie Lee Mullock (9)
Belle Vale Primary School, Belle Vale

Sadness . . .

Sadness is blue like Everton
Sadness sounds like a whale crying
Sadness tastes like water
Sadness feels like wet water
Sadness looks like the sky
Sadness smells like salt
Sadness reminds me of darkness.

Callum Jones (8)
Belle Vale Primary School, Belle Vale

Happiness

Happiness is yellow like the sun
Happiness tastes like cake
Happiness sounds like laughter
Happiness smells like strawberries
Happiness looks like fun
Happiness feels great
Happiness reminds me of my birthday.

Lauren Buckley (9)
Belle Vale Primary School, Belle Vale

Anger

Anger is the colour red like flames.
It reminds me of bad times.
It looks like she or he's angry.
It tastes like a bad time.
It feels bad.
It sounds like a bad time.

Melissa Mooney (9)
Belle Vale Primary School, Belle Vale

Love Is . . .

Love is red like a rose.
Love sounds like a sweet lovebird tweeting.
Love tastes like a kiss of joy.
Love feels like a newborn baby.
Love looks like a dark red heart.
Love smells like chocolate cookies.
Love reminds me of my boyfriend.

Chloe Campbell (8)
Belle Vale Primary School, Belle Vale

What Love Is Like . . .

Love is as red as a rose.
Love sounds like the waves whooshing in the sea.
Love tastes like juicy fruit.
Love feels like a round petal.
Love looks like singing birds.
Love smells like ice cream.
Love reminds you of your family and pets.

Emma Malins (7)
Belle Vale Primary School, Belle Vale

Love Is Like . . .

Love is the colour of pink like a pink flower.
Love is the sound of birds cheeping away.
Love tastes like a chocolate from a candy box.
Love feels like a soft, cuddly, teddy bear.
Love looks like kissing under the mistletoe.
Love smells like the wind on a windy day.

Jamielee Zwart (8)
Belle Vale Primary School, Belle Vale

Love

Love is bright pink like a Valentine's card.
Love sounds like birds tweeting.
Love tastes like a Swiss roll.
Love smells like fresh roses from the ground.
Love looks like a new view outside with you snuggled up with someone you love.
Love feels like petals falling from a tree of roses.
Love reminds me of a fun day out with my family for dinner in warm and sunny Spain.

Bobbi-Jo Banks (10)
Belle Vale Primary School, Belle Vale

Love Is . . .

Love is as red as a rose.
Love sounds like a heart thumping.
Love tastes like chocolates in a heart-shaped box.
Love feels like the wind.
Love looks like kissing under a tree.
Love smells like a beautiful bird gliding through the air.
Love reminds you of the last time you hugged your mum.

Danielle Jones (8)
Belle Vale Primary School, Belle Vale

Anger Is . . .

Anger is shadowy black in the night.
Anger sounds like stamping.
Anger tastes like a fizzy cola bottle.
Anger feels like thunder.
Anger looks like fire.
Anger smells like fire.
Anger reminds me of a big iceberg.

Amy Burns (7)
Belle Vale Primary School, Belle Vale

Happiness In Me

Happiness is crimson red like a bunch of fresh roses.
Happiness sounds like birds singing beautifully in the morning.
Happiness tastes like rich, soft, toffee pudding and a
hint of cinnamon.
Happiness smells like perfume moving towards me.
Happiness looks like a happy family all together and laughing.
Happiness feels like flowers growing gracefully inside me.
Happiness reminds me of celebrations and compliments.

Sarah Kathryn Bacon (10)
Belle Vale Primary School, Belle Vale

Silence

Silence is grey like a cloud on a stormy day
Silence sounds like a graveyard at night
Silence tastes like soggy chillis
Silence smells like a trash can full of rotting garbage
Silence looks like grey water
Silence feels like an empty grave
Silence reminds me of children asleep.

Dylan Butler (11)
Belle Vale Primary School, Belle Vale

Love Is . . .

Love is red like a rose
Love sounds like birds singing in the sky
Love tastes like a wedding cake
Love feels like a smooth apple
Love looks like a shining *star!*

Rebecca Rigby (7)
Belle Vale Primary School, Belle Vale

Funny Laughter

Laughter is yellow like a chick in its nest.
Laughter sounds like children playing in the park.
Laughter tastes like sweet strawberries freshly picked and washed.
Laughter smells like daisies and honey.
Laughter looks like a handsome hunk approaching my way.
Laughter feels like someone is telling a funny joke.
Laughter reminds me of playing with my bestest friends.

Alabama Bear-Wheatley (10)
Belle Vale Primary School, Belle Vale

Laughter

Laugher is orange like the sun.
Laughter sounds like people having a good time.
Laughter tastes like something cooked just right.
Laughter smells like roses freshly grown.
Laughter looks like people having a good time.
Laughter sounds like great fun with people screaming with laughter.
Laughter reminds me of good times.
Ha, ha, ha!

Georgia Rose (9)
Belle Vale Primary School, Belle Vale

Anger

Anger is dark green like a dirty pond
Anger sounds like horrible times
Anger tastes like burnt fish
Anger smells like fire burning
Anger looks like a fat monster
Anger feels like rock-hard mountains
It reminds me of bad times.

Matthew John Squires (10)
Belle Vale Primary School, Belle Vale

Fun, Yeah

Fun is bright pink like a skipping rope.
Fun sounds like people having a good time at the fair.
Fun tastes like candyfloss in the summer.
Fun is like summer flowers spreading all around.
Fun looks like I'm going to Mexico to go in the pool.
Fun feels like your heart beating so fast you can't move.
Fun reminds me of laughing every minute.

Hollie Rainford (10)
Belle Vale Primary School, Belle Vale

Happiness Is . . .

Happiness is green as a leaf,
Happiness sounds like a bird's singing,
Happiness tastes like a cake,
Happiness feels like a star,
Happiness looks like a rose in a red vase,
Happiness smells like a garden full of flowers,
Happiness reminds me of my birthday.

Beth Ashworth (8)
Belle Vale Primary School, Belle Vale

Happiness Is . . .

Happiness is yellow like a sun shining in sight,
Happiness sounds like a world full of wonderful things,
Happiness tastes like a sweet yellow apple,
Happiness feels like butterflies surrounding your way,
Happiness looks like 1,000 big yellow balloons,
Happiness smells like a big red rose,
Happiness reminds me of my old home.

Robyn Mulloy (8)
Belle Vale Primary School, Belle Vale

Happiness Is . . .

Happiness is as yellow as a sunflower,
Happiness sounds like a dog barking,
Happiness tastes like a prawn cracker,
Happiness feels like sand running through your hands,
Happiness looks like a hot dog,
Happiness smells like water throwing waves on the sand
and the shells,
Happiness reminds me of my mum and dad going away.

Erik Lindon (8)
Belle Vale Primary School, Belle Vale

Fear Is Frightening

Fear is dark blue like a big blueberry
Fear sounds like thunder in the sky
Fear tastes like a hot chilli pepper
Fear is like terror in my tummy
Fear looks like a monster in a hurry
Fear smells like a burnt piece of toast
Fear reminds me of a jack-in-the box.

Georgia Fahy (7)
Belle Vale Primary School, Belle Vale

Anger Is . . .

Anger is red like a burning fire.
Anger sounds like an exploding volcano.
Anger tastes like a poisonous apple.
Anger feels like someone hitting me.
Anger looks like a burning sun.
Anger smells like fire.
Anger reminds me of a river of lava.

Luke Alben (8)
Belle Vale Primary School, Belle Vale

Anger Is . . .

Anger is red like a fire.
Anger sounds like a dust tornado.
Anger tastes like a chilli pepper.
Anger feels like a fire in your belly.
Anger looks like a burning red sun.
Anger smells like smoke from a fire.
Anger reminds me of fighting with my brothers.

Rachel Daye (7)
Belle Vale Primary School, Belle Vale

Love Is . . .

Love is pink like a rose
Love sounds like your heart beating
Love tastes like a bee buzzing in your mouth
Love feels like the sea hitting the shore
Love looks like millions of hearts floating in the air
Love smells like one hundred flowers in a field
Love reminds you of when you've reached out for someone's hand.

Robyn Hughes (8)
Belle Vale Primary School, Belle Vale

Anger Is . . .

Anger is red like a juicy cherry.
Anger sounds like shouting through your mind.
Anger tastes like fiery chillies.
Anger feels like tearing something apart.
Anger smells like smoky steam.
Anger reminds you of all the nasty things you've done.

Emily Campbell (8)
Belle Vale Primary School, Belle Vale

Sadness Is . . .

Sadness is blue like a ball
Sadness sounds like the big waves swishing
Sadness tastes like dry bread
Sadness feels like a burning fire
Sadness looks like damp cloves
Sadness smells like old bin bags
Sadness reminds me of when I broke my arm.

Holly Middlebrough (8)
Belle Vale Primary School, Belle Vale

Love Is . . .

Love is the colour of red roses.
Love sounds like music.
Love tastes like red cherries.
Love feels like the sea.
Love looks like roses.
Love smells like mints.
Love reminds me of the sun.

Abigail Smith (7)
Belle Vale Primary School, Belle Vale

Autumn

Mixed-up leaves with colours
Red, green and yellow
Coming off the big dead tree.
People's feet stepping like a knight fighting his way
Through spiky thorns.
Wind whooshing all the leaves backwards
Like a swirling, whirling hurricane.
The smell of dead leaves
And the farmer's manure.

Jessica Brownless (8)
Ingleby Mill Primary School, Stockton-on-Tees

Feelings

Writhing inside me
I'm filled with emotions
Never noticed it before
I'm filled with the power to feel

Feelings are flowing inside me
Emotions in every inch of my body
Love
Hatred
Happiness
Every one is there!

Laura McCann (8)
Ingleby Mill Primary School, Stockton-on-Tees

Silence

Silence
White like a snowflake drifting
Like still air
Feeling of peace on Earth
No worry
Taste of cake icing
No one living.

Rebecca Boston (8)
Ingleby Mill Primary School, Stockton-on-Tees

Happiness

Pink like a rosebud blooming into a shimmering flower.
A bird twittering in the air.
The fresh air floating around.
Crispy chocolate cake, warm out of the oven.
A kitten curling up on my lap.

Sophie Shelton (8)
Ingleby Mill Primary School, Stockton-on-Tees

Happiness

Yellow, the sun is shining brightly in the sky.
Like dribbling sweat coming down your face.
Tweeting chicks coming out of their shells
And robin redbreasts singing in the air.
Sizzling barbecues and sausages on the barbecues.
Soft ice drinks lying in the bright sun shimmering in the light.
As the glittering sun goes down and the shining moon and stars
come out for the long dark night.

Molly Tudor (7)
Ingleby Mill Primary School, Stockton-on-Tees

Anger . . .

Dark red like fire
Shooting from a dragon's nostrils.
Screaming parents when you're in trouble.
Very sticky saliva from your mouth.
Smells of a dead human brain.
People dying in a fierce war.
Something exploding inside you.

Louis Clapham (8)
Ingleby Mill Primary School, Stockton-on-Tees

Anger

Dark red like fiery blood coming from a hammerhead shark.
Drum from a football stadium,
Nasty sound for the away side!
Red-hot chilli peppers burning my tongue.
Red lava coming out of a volcano.

Samuel Candlin (8)
Ingleby Mill Primary School, Stockton-on-Tees

Hunger

A slave who only gets a litre of water and an apple a day,
Starving till death,
Making you fall asleep,
You can taste sick,
You can only smell food,
Making you imagine a bowl of fruit,
You grow so thin that you can see your bones,
You know that death is around the corner.

Toby Flack (8)
Ingleby Mill Primary School, Stockton-on-Tees

Anger

Dark red like blood from a dead body
Like horror going through my spine
Tastes like flesh from a dead man
Sounds like a man being murdered
Makes me feel like I'm being ripped
Smells like eyeballs all crushed up
Reminds me of dead bodies in Hell.

Aaron Wiggett (7)
Ingleby Mill Primary School, Stockton-on-Tees

Happiness

Pink like strawberry ice cream slowly melting in the blazing sun,
Screaming fireworks making light pictures,
Fresh bread from the oven,
Jam roly-poly from the oven with dripping custard,
The warm, cosy bedcovers warming me up as I settle in bed.

Lyndon Davies (8)
Ingleby Mill Primary School, Stockton-on-Tees

Anger

Fiery red like hot blood.
Like a roaring lion getting his prey.
It feels like fire burning in my stomach
As if a dragon is trapped in it.
A sword from a wounded warrior.
It feels like my heart is broken.
Like gone-off milk.
I feel like I could explode.
It reminds me of a dead body.
Tastes like smoke from a fire or
When someone punches you.

Samantha Readman (8)
Ingleby Mill Primary School, Stockton-on-Tees

Anger

Red is like fire
Breathing from a dragon.
It feels like a volcano
Flooding the Earth.
It reminds me of blood.
Sounds like my cousin crying loudly.
Smells like an oven burning bread.

Eleanor Thornton (8)
Ingleby Mill Primary School, Stockton-on-Tees

Happiness

Gold like seeing a trophy in the sun.
Sizzling bacon in a pan.
Hot fresh petrol from the petrol tank
Spag Bol any time from the oven.
I feel how cute a newborn puppy is with its mum.

Alfie Jenkins (7)
Ingleby Mill Primary School, Stockton-on-Tees

Darkness

Darkness is black like a midnight sky.
It sounds like a howling wolf, ready to pounce on its prey.
Darkness tastes like a cold ice lolly melting on my tongue.
Darkness smells like the smoke from a burning candle.
It looks like a blanket of coal.
It feels like the world closing in on me.
It reminds me of a hot pan full of bubbly gravy.

Holly Alderton (8)
Ingleby Mill Primary School, Stockton-on-Tees

Anger

Anger is red like a dragon's fiery eyes.
It sounds like the *bang!* of a volcano.
Anger tastes like spicy popcorn chicken.
Anger smells like the smoke from a fire.
It looks like the Earth's core, full of fire and terror.
Anger feels like a sword in your heart.
Anger reminds me of a dragon in a castle.

Jack Medforth (8)
Ingleby Mill Primary School, Stockton-on-Tees

Spring

Gold like the sun shining brightly in the sky.
Feels like leaves falling on the ground gently.
Sounds like silence in the garden and street.
Smells like a spring cake warming in the oven.
Reminds me of a land made of beautiful roses and tulips.

Nieve Walton-O'Brien (7)
Ingleby Mill Primary School, Stockton-on-Tees

Anger

Red like a volcano.
Like breathing fire.
Feeling like I am going to explode.
Tasting like a hot chilli.
Like I am going to burst.
Like a dead body.

Joshua Farmer (8)
Ingleby Mill Primary School, Stockton-on-Tees

Hunger

Sounds like a bear roaring
Feels like you're empty
Dark as a tunnel
Looks as if you aren't born
A half-built house
Ready to be fed.

Lydia McCann (8)
Ingleby Mill Primary School, Stockton-on-Tees

What Am I?

Red as a fireball
Fast as light
Spinning round and round
Light as a pencil
Up and down on my finger.

Harry Hornby (8)
Ingleby Mill Primary School, Stockton-on-Tees

Doom

Darkness like the midnight sky.
A cloak of doom.
Very gloomy grave.
A burnt human.
Lots and lots of dragons.
Lost in the deepest forest.
One dead eagle.

Charlie Sewell (8)
Ingleby Mill Primary School, Stockton-on-Tees

Happiness

Hot chocolate melting in the oven.
A race with all your friends.
Going down a water park slide.
Licking a vanilla ice cream.
A burger on a barbecue.
The smell of treacle cake.

Bradley Moore (8)
Ingleby Mill Primary School, Stockton-on-Tees

Happiness

Pink like feeling happy.
It sounds like birds singing in the tree.
It is the beautiful smell in the oven.
Hot melting fudge dripping from my spoon.
My dog licking my face.

Harry Bennett (8)
Ingleby Mill Primary School, Stockton-on-Tees

Darkness

Darkness is black like the fur of a wolf.
It sounds like the howling of a wolf.
It tastes like black mints melting in my mouth.
It smells like grey salty air.
It looks like the outline of a bear.
It feels like a heavy weight.
It reminds me of a bloodthirsty bat.

Christopher Ayre (8)
Ingleby Mill Primary School, Stockton-on-Tees

Anger

Dark red like fire
Shooting from a dragon's nostrils.
Screaming parents when you're in trouble.
Blood when I bite my tongue.
Burning from the oven.
Punching myself when angry.

Megan Calvert (8)
Ingleby Mill Primary School, Stockton-on-Tees

Happiness

White like snowdrops swaying in the wind
The sound of someone fixing the broken TV
The smell of sizzling bacon in the frying pan
Lovely white chocolate from Tesco
Like a dog licking me on the hand.

James Lyth (8)
Ingleby Mill Primary School, Stockton-on-Tees

Darkness

Darkness is black like a pitch-black night.
It sounds like wind howling with no bright lights.
Darkness tastes like an icy-cold ice cube.
Darkness smells like a freezer.
It looks like the Earth is pitch-black.
Darkness feels like a wolf's hair.
Darkness reminds me of a dark black bear hunting its prey.

Zhuhaa Siddiq (8)
Ingleby Mill Primary School, Stockton-on-Tees

Happiness

Orange like the sun
Feels like fire burning in my mouth
Sounds like birds tweeting in the trees
Reminds me of the light blue sky
Smells like a blob of water all over me.

Tyler Hersi (8)
Ingleby Mill Primary School, Stockton-on-Tees

Happiness

Pink like strawberry ice cream melting in the sun.
Somebody playing peaceful music on a piano.
Hot sizzling burgers from the barbecue.
My mum's home-made chocolate cake.
My teddy when I cuddle up to him at night.

Dominic Wheatley (8)
Ingleby Mill Primary School, Stockton-on-Tees

Anger!

Anger is red like a mischievous devil.
It sounds like a lion roaring in my ears.
Anger tastes like red-hot chilli peppers and fire in my mouth.
It smells like burning wood from a bonfire.
It looks like a fire-breathing dragon.
It feels like steam coming through my ears and fire in my eyes.
Anger reminds me of a volcano just about to explode.

Lewis Heap (7)
Ingleby Mill Primary School, Stockton-on-Tees

Anger

Anger is red like a blazing fire.
It sounds like wood crackling.
Anger tastes like a red-hot oven.
Anger smells like something burning.
It looks like a fire-breathing dragon.
Anger feels like hot tomatoes.
Anger reminds me of someone angry.

Joe Savage (8)
Ingleby Mill Primary School, Stockton-on-Tees

Dolphins

We swim around the ocean,
We move in one fast motion,
When we decide to eat, it's fish that we will choose,
We have a rubber body, which keeps us safe,
We have a swishing tail with fins that help us to swim,
We like to jump in the sea and blow bubbles under the water.

Eve Horrocks (8)
Ingleby Mill Primary School, Stockton-on-Tees

Happiness

Happiness is light blue like a lit-up sky.
It sounds like water pouring from a tap.
Happiness tastes like a tingle in your throat.
Happiness smells like a sweet mint.
It looks like a huge bar of Galaxy chocolate.
Happiness feels like a soft comfortable pillow.
Happiness reminds me of my best friend's party.

Rebecca Warren (8)
Ingleby Mill Primary School, Stockton-on-Tees

Anger

Anger is red like an exploding volcano.
It's like molten rocks smashing on the ground.
Anger tastes like hot chillis flaring in my mouth.
Anger smells like overcooked bacon.
It looks like lava blasting out of my ears.
Anger feels like a water bomb hitting me.
Anger reminds me of enormous volcanoes.

Thomas Dalton (7)
Ingleby Mill Primary School, Stockton-on-Tees

Happiness

Gold like a trophy meaning victory in the sun
Like sweet music to my heart
Fish finger butties fresh from the oven
Fryer Tuck's delectable prawn crackers
A dog waking up in its bed.

Robert Purcell (8)
Ingleby Mill Primary School, Stockton-on-Tees

Love

Love is red like a frilly, beautiful dress.
Love sounds like angels singing as I sleep.
Love tastes like wedding cake ready to erupt in my mouth.
Love smells like fresh bread, just out of the oven.
Love looks like a boy and a girl . . . then comes a baby,
what a happy family!
Love feels like warm air surrounding me, keeping my body warm.
Love reminds me of my mum and dad's first kiss in the sunset.

Rebecca Hopson (8)
Ingleby Mill Primary School, Stockton-on-Tees

Sadness

Sadness is grey like a shaking miserable darkness.
It sounds like rain dropping in a huge flooding puddle.
Sadness tastes like tornadoes sweeping through England.
Sadness smells like storms of thunder and lightning.
It looks like stars dropping down from the sky.
Sadness feels like shivering on cold wet days.
Sadness reminds me of floating away in a deep dark sleep.

Adam Stephenson (8)
Ingleby Mill Primary School, Stockton-on-Tees

Anger

Anger is red like a scaly dragon.
Anger sounds like a dangerous cobra hissing.
Anger tastes like steam burning my tongue.
Anger smells like a flaring red fire.
Anger looks like a scary shark.
Anger feels like a big brown volcano.
Anger reminds me of frightening Roman soldiers.

Jonathan Glew (8)
Ingleby Mill Primary School, Stockton-on-Tees

Anger!

Anger is red like a groaning monster.
It sounds like a stomping beast.
Anger tastes like flesh from a dead animal.
Anger smells like a dirty old bear.
It looks like a red bull going to charge at me.
It feels like strong boulders on a cliff.
Anger reminds me of Celts charging at their enemies.

Tom Dodds (8)
Ingleby Mill Primary School, Stockton-on-Tees

Love!

Love is pink like a beautiful love heart.
It sounds like the tweeting of a gliding bird.
It tastes like chocolate melting in my mouth.
It smells like Yorkshire puddings on a fresh dinner.
It looks like people hugging each other.
Love feels like a great wedding.
Love reminds me of beauty.

Charley Roberts (8)
Ingleby Mill Primary School, Stockton-on-Tees

Darkness

Darkness is black and muddy like a shoe has just stamped on me.
It sounds like a scared girl screaming.
Darkness tastes like hot meat that is chewy to eat.
Darkness smells like the smoke of a candle just blown out.
It looks like hot gravy bubbling in my pot.
Darkness feels like dark chocolate.
It reminds me of a ghost train!

Lucy Thomas (8)
Ingleby Mill Primary School, Stockton-on-Tees

Love

Love is pink like a frilly wedding dress.
Love sounds like mermaids singing and dancing in the ocean.
Love tastes like twinkly stars tickling my tongue.
Love smells like a fresh loaf of bread from the oven.
Love looks like a pink heart full of joy.
Love feels like flowers blooming in the meadows.
Love reminds me of weddings and flowers.

Gabrielle Poole (8)
Ingleby Mill Primary School, Stockton-on-Tees

Fun

Fun is orange like a basketball.
It sounds like the silver-orange ball is shining.
It tastes like it is blazing.
It smells like the sky is moving.
It looks like children playing football.
It feels like my heart is going up and down.
It reminds me of my PlayStation.

Kieran Mulroy (7)
Ingleby Mill Primary School, Stockton-on-Tees

Love

Love is like a pretty rose.
It sounds like my heart beating very fast.
Love tastes like sweet hearts floating through my body.
Love smells like lavender up your nose.
It looks like sparkling dust floating through the air.
It feels like something tickling my heart.
Love reminds me of my family.

Sarah Donnelly (7)
Ingleby Mill Primary School, Stockton-on-Tees

Love

Love is red like beautiful hearts.
It sounds like someone is giving you a hug.
Love tastes like sweet red strawberries soaking in my mouth.
Love smells like lovely pink roses in your garden.
It looks like pink fluffy candyfloss, all ready to eat.
Love feels like you are pink all over.
Love reminds me of my heart beating fast.

Sophie Spoor (8)
Ingleby Mill Primary School, Stockton-on-Tees

Anger

Anger is red like an erupting volcano.
It sounds like steam coming out of my ears.
Anger tastes like I've swallowed fire.
It smells like a blazing fire.
Anger looks like I'm a huge red face.
It feels like I am going to burst.
It reminds me of a fire-breathing dragon.

Elliott Wilson (8)
Ingleby Mill Primary School, Stockton-on-Tees

Sadness

Sadness is grey like a heavy cloud.
It sounds like dripping tears from your eyes.
It tastes like a salty sea.
It smells like a smelly boot.
It looks like a grave where someone has died.
It feels like a handful of tears.

Aimée Smith (7)
Ingleby Mill Primary School, Stockton-on-Tees

Anger

Anger is black like a wet, dark cave under the earth.
It sounds like a bear that's hungry for food.
Anger tastes like you have lava running down your throat.
Anger smells like a volcano has erupted.
It looks like a dragon is ready to breathe his dangerous fire.
Anger feels like you are going to burst.
Anger reminds me of trees that have been set on fire.

Katie Taylor (8)
Ingleby Mill Primary School, Stockton-on-Tees

Sadness

Sadness is black like the shadows in the night,
It sounds like the crying of a baby,
Sadness tastes like a small grape,
Sadness smells like bitter lemons,
Sadness feels like dull colours rushing through me,
Sadness reminds me of a bullied child.

Saurabh Sharma (7)
Ingleby Mill Primary School, Stockton-on-Tees

Love

Love is either red or pink, like a big love heart.
Love sounds like two inseparable people laughing together.
Love tastes like sweet, Thornton's chocolate.
Love smells like red roses.
Love looks like your eyes are smitten.
Love feels like your knees go weak at the joints, so much that you nearly faint.
Love reminds me of two people connecting with their emotions.

Sharni Wright (11)
Marlborough Road Primary School, Salford

Anger

Anger is a dark rage of fire.
It is a dark, deep hole in the centre of the Earth.
It sounds like a roaring noise and you can't see
where it's coming from.
It tastes like a hard piece of bone.
It smells like the smelliest skunk in a dump.
It looks like a dark hole straight through the Earth.
It feels like a rough rock on fire in my hand.
It reminds you of being in a dark,
Mystical hole, in the middle of nowhere.

Damian Swift (11)
Marlborough Road Primary School, Salford

Anger

Anger is the colour of red like a furious fire.
Anger sounds like a lion's roar when it's about to pounce on its prey.
Anger tastes like a red-hot vindaloo.
Anger smells like a burnt sofa that has just been put out.
Anger looks like a heart on fire.
Anger feels like a bomb has just been set off inside you.
Anger reminds me of a scary ghost moving in me.

Victoria Emily Walker (11)
Marlborough Road Primary School, Salford

My Nieces

My nieces fill my heart with joy just by looking at them.
They are as nice and generous as a box of chocolates.
They are always happy, it fills my heart with burning joy.
They are like a burning sun, always laughing with the tickles I bring,
But there's one thing I know, our happiness and love will never *end!*

Nicole McNeill (11)
Marlborough Road Primary School, Salford

Loneliness

Loneliness is plain white, like a blank page.
Loneliness sounds like you're all on your own,
As if you're in outer space, nothing to be seen.
Loneliness tastes like pure, plain water,
Not like a great, gigantic fruit dish.
It smells like you're in a cold, damp room all on your own.
It looks like there's no features on your face.
It feels like your heart is broken and never can be fixed again.

It may remind you of when you're left on your own!

Hateema Zia (11)
Marlborough Road Primary School, Salford

My Mum

As soft as a teddy bear,
Warm and cuddly and always there.
As bright as a yellow smiley face,
Which reminds me of the laughter we have together,
On a green field, searching for four-leafed clovers.
The red colour of her heart,
And how it holds so much love.
Absolute happiness that she brings.

Holly Crawshaw (11)
Marlborough Road Primary School, Salford

My Grandad

As soft and as pink as a clown's face,
But still prickly as a pineapple.
A bright green meadow full of lucky green clovers.
As red as his nose when he had a cold but still full with love
deep down.

Chelsea Kinsley (11)
Marlborough Road Primary School, Salford

Sadness

Sadness is blue like the dark blue sea.
Sadness sounds like teardrops that fall from you to me.
Sadness looks like a dark black hole.
Sadness tastes like plain, black, dirty coal.
Sadness smells like dead human flesh that's been there for years.
Sadness could flood the world with all the human tears.
Sadness reminds me of a lost friend
And all the good times that came to an end.

Princess Adegbite (11)
Marlborough Road Primary School, Salford

Fear

Fear is black like a ghost creeping around a haunted castle,
annoying people and causing hassle.
Fear sounds like a creaking door opening with a squeak.
Fear tastes like rotten flesh that's been rotting for a week.
Fear smells like a scary cell with nowhere to sit.
Fear looks like a dark cave with no living creatures in it.
Fear feels like a hard rock that has never been broken.
Fear is like the horrible secrets that should never be spoken.

Quynh Hoang (11)
Marlborough Road Primary School, Salford

Love

Love is red like hearts filled with joy.
Love sounds like a heart beating for its charm.
Love tastes like a box of chocolates.
Love smells like a bunch of roses.
Love looks like a couple in love.
Love feels like something that you will never let go.
Love reminds people of how they love each other so much.

Hana Ahmed Jibril (11)
Marlborough Road Primary School, Salford

Quickly

Quickly, the cheetah pounces into the wood,
Quickly, the runner ran as fast as he could,
Quickly, the rocket zooms to the stars,
Quickly, the motorbike overtakes cars!

Quickly, the train rushes down the lane,
Quickly, the plane goes high above the rain,
Quickly, the vicious spider catches a fly,
As the peregrine falcon flaps goodbye!

Daniel Sant (9)
Puss Bank Primary School, Macclesfield

Silence

Silence is white like a soft fluffy cloud floating in the sky.
It feels like my dad's soft, silky tie.
It reminds me of lots of birds that can fly.
It looks like a stadium after a rugby game live.
It smells like my lunch at dinner time.
It tastes like a yummy piece of blueberry pie.
It sounds like someone about to cry.

Emma Welton (9)
Puss Bank Primary School, Macclesfield

Anger

Anger is red as a forest fire blazing through the open bush.
It looks like a huge, red-hot flaming torch,
It smells like a raging fire going on and on,
It feels like a boiling kettle about to explode,
It sounds like a huge giant roaring,
It reminds me of something just waiting, waiting to go wrong,
It tastes like twenty red-hot chilli peppers all in my mouth at once!

Peter Griffen (9)
Puss Bank Primary School, Macclesfield

I Didn't Come To School Because . . .

I didn't come to school because I was sick from eating
too much ice cream.
I didn't come to school because I went on holiday.
I didn't come to school because I was at a football match.
I didn't come to school because C Ronaldo invited me to his house.
I didn't come to school because there was a black hole
next to my bed.
I didn't come to school because there was a spider on
my door handle.
I didn't come to school because I got lost in the bath.
I didn't come to school because aliens took my school uniform.
I didn't come to school because two men in gorilla costumes
kidnapped me!

Gabrielle Sinclair & Ross Patterson (9)
Puss Bank Primary School, Macclesfield

Fun

Fun is yellow like the golden sun and the wave of the sweet daffodils.
It reminds me of a sunny free day when you are playing with
your friends.
It looks like a big funfair with lots of games and stalls.
It tastes like a mouth-watering ice cream all creamy with chocolate
sauce on top.
It feels like a joyful day out at a National Trust property in the
bright sunshine.
It smells like a rose flowering in the spring in my back garden.
It sounds like a disco with very loud pop music.

Amy Warrington (9)
Puss Bank Primary School, Macclesfield

I Didn't Wear My School Shoes

I didn't wear my school shoes because I forgot them.
I didn't wear my school shoes because I couldn't find them.
I didn't wear my school shoes because they fell down Niagara Falls.
I didn't wear my school shoes because Lord Voldemort put a spell on them and they disappeared.
I didn't wear my school shoes because I jumped on them and they blew up.
I didn't wear my school shoes because little Martians used them as beds.

Sam Goulden & Luke Robertson (9)
Puss Bank Primary School, Macclesfield

Love

Love is pink like a soft, fluffy, tasty, plump, puffy candyfloss.
It looks like a big cloud that's swaying in the wind and about to toss.
It sounds like a beating heart being wrapped in a warm blanket.
It reminds me of my mum when she gives me a hug.
It smells like melting chocolate, nice and brown, nearly ready to eat.
It feels like a cushion just plumped up and feathers falling
on my nose.
It tastes like a Minstrel melting in my mouth.

Charlotte Dean (9)
Puss Bank Primary School, Macclesfield

I Didn't Do My Homework

I didn't do my homework because I dropped it in a puddle.
I didn't do my homework because when I was going to have a bath I tripped and it fell in the loo.
I didn't do my homework because James Bond came to my house, stole it and chucked it off the Empire State Building.
I didn't do my homework because my guinea pig turned into a giant and ate it.

Joe Lawson (9)
Puss Bank Primary School, Macclesfield

Silence

Silence is normal white like a church mouse.
It feels like an empty nothingness.
It looks like dust floating past a room.
It reminds me of death when a body is cremated in the
burning flames.
It tastes like thick cream in a dreamy heaven.
It sounds like a hole, one thousand feet down.
It smells like cheese alone on a plate.

Ryan Ward (9)
Puss Bank Primary School, Macclesfield

Love

Love is blue like the silent, wavy, big sea.
It reminds me of a picture of a shiny red heart.
It feels like a heart pounding inside me.
It tastes like a chocolate filled with red strawberry cream.
It sounds like birds that fly in the sky singing.
It looks like the bright shiny sun that sets and rises with loveliness.
It smells like the early fresh breeze.

Darren Smith (9)
Puss Bank Primary School, Macclesfield

Love

Love is pink like a lovely hot chocolate filling.
It tastes like a creamy Minstrel.
It looks like a happy couple.
It feels like you are in a dream.
It sounds like a cat purring.
It smells like flowers swaying in the breeze.
It reminds me of when I was a baby.

Conor Gibney (8)
Puss Bank Primary School, Macclesfield

Anger

Anger is red like the second hottest, driest planet - Mars.
It feels like all of the bumps on Pluto.
It tastes like the food shortage on the moon.
It looks like the blazing fires of Mercury.
It smells like the emptiness of space.
It reminds me of a black hole waiting to open.

Nicola Ratcliffe (8)
Puss Bank Primary School, Macclesfield

My Dad's Motorbike

My dad's motorbike is a Ducati,
It sounds like a monster to me,
It roars and it growls like a tiger,
But it doesn't scare me!

He wears leathers and a shiny black helmet,
And he goes down the street like a rocket!
Rides up to the Cat and Fiddle for a beer,
He comes back down the hill with no fear!

Ria Horsley (10)
St Barnabas' CE Primary School, Macclesfield

All Alone

I'm all alone on the wide, wide sea,
It's all dark, here comes a shark,
Looking for something to eat which is meat.
All alone under the dark, dark sea.
So scared, no one here to accompany me.
I'm always alone.

Sabrina Khan (11)
St Barnabas' CE Primary School, Macclesfield

Why?

Why are things so easy?
Why are things so hard?
Why is everything so nice?
Why is everything so miserable and boring?
What causes it?

Feelings!

Sad, happy, mad, bad, are all these feelings,
Happy means joyful,
Bad means horrible,
What is the cause?

Feelings!

Why am I happy when I'm sad?
Why does my head feel like a bouncing ball?
Why does my tummy feel like a washing machine swirling around
making a really loud sound?

What causes it?

Feelings!

Megan Morgan (9)
St Barnabas' CE Primary School, Macclesfield

Jealousy

I'm jealous of you
I'm jealous of her
Everyone has some jealousy
A burning pain in your stomach
A throbbing pain in your throat
A red-hot dragon curling round your body
Injuries happen in your head
Jealously is a virus you just can't control
Once jealousy's got you there's no escape
So don't let it catch you in the first place.

Charlotte Dale (10)
St Barnabas' CE Primary School, Macclesfield

My Best Friend

He makes me happy when I'm sad.
He makes me laugh with joy.
He plays with me when I feel lonely.
He is very sporty.
People think he is a good role model.
He plays for the football team.
His name screams with fun.
Ben Pritchard is his name.

Brandon Healey (10)
St Barnabas' CE Primary School, Macclesfield

Food

Food is scrummy,
It fills my tummy
And it's really yummy

I like jelly,
When I'm watching telly
And it fills my belly

When I'm hungry,
I need food
Otherwise I'm in a mood.

Hannah Holloway (11)
St Barnabas' CE Primary School, Macclesfield

Frustration

When I am frustrated I walk away
I try not to go out and play
When I am frustrated I go and sit down
And I try and get rid of my frown
When I am frustrated I see a fire burning
When I am frustrated I hear metal churning.

Ben Pritchard (11)
St Barnabas' CE Primary School, Macclesfield

Mixed Feelings

Why is everything in life so boring?
Why do things make me feel sad?
I love it when I'm happy,
But I don't when I'm bad.

When I'm feeling lonely,
I cry and cry,
I just want to die,
I say to myself.
So let's just pray,
That one day,
Our loneliness dies away.

Sometimes I'm happy,
Because my troubles have gone,
But that's what life's about,
Being happy one moment,
And sad the next.

What do you feel like today?
Joyful, happy sad,
Or even mad!

Aliya Saddique (10)
St Barnabas' CE Primary School, Macclesfield

Poems

Poems getting rhymier, rhymier,
They get rhythm from nothing.
So when writing poems don't do it!
Because they are hard to rhyme,
Try writing about friends,
Example, friends are really great.

Thomas Amanis (10)
St Barnabas' CE Primary School, Macclesfield

Why Am I Angry?

Why am I angry?
Why am I sad?
Why am I grumpy
And always bad?
There's just one thing
I cannot stop,
Those silly noises.
I scream and I beam.
In this silly block of mine
Everything is just fine.
But then I blow
Oh no . . .
Off I go . . . !

Ashly Millington (11)
St Barnabas' CE Primary School, Macclesfield

Moose

Moose are brown
Moose have fur
They're so cool
You have to concur.

Moose have antlers
All different shapes
They could even be
Your best mate!

Joshua Stanway (10)
St Barnabas' CE Primary School, Macclesfield

Why Me?

When someone dies you feel empty inside,
you feel something is missing
so you start wishing,
you wish for them back
but they've gone into the black
and they're
never
coming
back!

Grace Currie (11)
St Barnabas' CE Primary School, Macclesfield

Nervous

Nervous
I am also sad
And I get so mad.
I will get so mad, I will turn to bad.
I get nervous when doing a test but sometimes I think
That I am the best of the rest, sometimes
I get in a mess and I go red in my head.

Thomas McMurdo (11)
St Barnabas' CE Primary School, Macclesfield

Friends

My friend's a best friend
My friend is forever
My friend is always there for me
When I need her
My friends are for life
All in all, my friends are the best.

Ellie Bennett (10)
St Barnabas' CE Primary School, Macclesfield

Save Our Planet

We want our corals,
We don't want a squabble.
Pollution will kill all our fish,
Is that your wish?

Then come the birds,
Mark my words.
Listen to this jive,
Keep them alive.

Under the sea,
We should keep the fish free.
Now don't you see?
Please listen to me.

This is the end,
If we don't start a trend.
We can help the fish survive,
Do you feel my jive?

Don't be part of the problem!
Stop pollution,
Be part of the solution.

Michael Moran (10)
St Bridget's Catholic Primary School, Warrington

We Need New Rules

The animals are in danger,
What can we do?
Keep them away from litter,
So they can have a healthy life.

The animals are in danger,
All these creatures in the world.
They do lots for us,
So let's keep them alive in the world.

The animals are in danger,
Just because of pollution.
We do not want this to happen,
So we need to come up with a solution.

We do not want to kill all the animals,
Because this will be cruel.
This will be a sad time,
So let's get a new rule.

'Save our animals,
Stop pollution!'

Sophie Brady (10)
St Bridget's Catholic Primary School, Warrington

Our Planet Is Cool

Our planet is cool
If you drop litter you will be a fool,
Oil spills, animals die
Lots of people start to cry.

I'm here to tell you one or two things
Which I hope make your head bell ring.

Our planet is cool
I love the fish in the sea
They swim so happily with glee,
Till a bad oil spill
From the big ships
These fish aren't any good
To even go with chips.

Our planet is cool
Sea otters die
That makes people cry,
All the trash comes out to play
But lots of people just say, 'Hey!'

Katie Gleave (10)
St Bridget's Catholic Primary School, Warrington

Spoiling The Planet

Litter, litter everywhere
Do not drop it anywhere.
Cans, paper, lolly sticks, plastic bags
Litter, litter everywhere
Do not drop it anywhere.
Sofas, tables, glass bottles, cigarettes
Litter, litter everywhere
Do not drop it anywhere
We seem not to care!

Jake Miller (10)
St Bridget's Catholic Primary School, Warrington

I Hate Pollution

I hate pollution,
Please save the ocean
The whales are dying,
I feel like crying.

I hate pollution
Please save the rivers,
The oil is spilling,
Please stop the killing.

I hate pollution
Please save the forest,
The tigers are on the run,
Running from the man with the gun!

I hate pollution
Please save the planet,
Pollution is ruining the sky,
Making the ice melt and the polar bears die.

Leah Green (10)
St Bridget's Catholic Primary School, Warrington

Our Beautiful Planet

The air pollution is really bad,
It makes everyone sick and sad,
Fumes off buses, cars and motorbikes,
Makes the air go really bad,
All the rubbish in the world,
It is so horrid it will take over the world.

The air pollution is still so bad,
It could kill us and our mums and dads,
As you see it is so bad,
So take our advice and be really glad,
Have a solution,
That we're trying to stop pollution,
We think we may.

Jaime Wright
St Bridget's Catholic Primary School, Warrington

Animals In Pollution

I want to save little fish
From evil pollution.
All the oil off the ships,
Polluting all the dolphins.

Living creatures in the sea,
All the sharks becoming extinct.
Seals breathe in the oil,
They will all drop down dead.

The coral reef in the water,
Will become polluted.
All the ducks eating the fish
Will become extinct.

Baby otters cruelly dying,
From the oil off the ships,
The birds diving down low,
Will die because of pollution.

Reece Smith (9)
St Bridget's Catholic Primary School, Warrington

Our Beautiful Planet

Our beautiful planet is being destroyed.
Why are we doing this to our beautiful planet?
Passive smoking,
Oil spills,
All this really kills,
So stop doing this to our beautiful planet.

Our beautiful planet is being destroyed
If we stop this murdering,
Our beautiful planet could be the planet of the future.
So stop all this murdering
And put a stop to the pollution
And save our beautiful planet.

Joseph Mountain (10)
St Bridget's Catholic Primary School, Warrington

The Environment

Our planet is cool
But dropping litter seems the new rule
Thinking about pollution
I'm begging to think we need a solution

Our planet is cool
But dropping litter seems the new rule
Oil spills, animals die
People start to cry

Our planet is cool
But dropping litter seems the new rule
They swim with glee
Then they die in the sea

Why do people think it's right to drop litter?
I just don't understand how they can be so bitter?

Karl Mahoney (9)
St Bridget's Catholic Primary School, Warrington

Stop Throwing Litter!

Stop throwing litter . . .
If you throw litter you are also killing our planet.
Think of little things such as fish,
Thousands of fish die every year because of us.

If you see someone throwing litter,
Then just tell him to put it in the nearest bin.
Our planet will be a lot safer then
For birds, fish, otters and others.

Things will look a lot prettier,
It will look like a dream come true,
With the sweet sound of birds singing
And the cool breeze making the colourful flowers flow,
So help save our planet!

Ellisha Hale (10)
St Bridget's Catholic Primary School, Warrington

Save Our Animals

Save our animals
Don't let them die
Save our animals
Or the end is nigh

Save our animals
Don't drop litter
Save our animals
Make them fitter

Save our animals
Cut the plastic
And if you do
That will be fantastic

Save our animals
Don't spill oil
Save our animals
Or the world will spoil

Save our animals
Do not cry
Save our animals
Don't let them die

Save our animals
Let them sleep
Save our animals
Let some leap.

Natalie-Louise Poole
St Bridget's Catholic Primary School, Warrington

Don't Let Them Die . . .

Animals near to their death,
Fish, otters and ducks.
They need to stay alive,
Don't let them die . . .

Animals near to their death,
Keep them away from litter.
Let's all save the animals,
Don't let them die . . .

Animals near to their death,
They are almost dead.
Let's all help the animals,
Don't let them die . . .

Animals near to their death,
Pollution is very bad.
Keep the animals away,
Don't let them die . . .

Animals near to their death,
Oil spills can kill.
Let's hope they stay alive,
Don't let them die!

Don't let them die because we're killing our planet.

Luke Boyd (10)
St Bridget's Catholic Primary School, Warrington

Environment Poem

I have dived
Into the hive
As I approached
The great white whale
Around the back there's the white mark.

This creature is beautiful
But you are pitiful
You're not helping
You are destroying.

The is dead annoying
Everything is depressing
But still we do nothing.

You are now helping
The fish are giggling with glee
You've helped the environment
Now say goodbye to me . . .

Oh not that was a dream
Things aren't what they seem
I thought you were helping the environment
Now everything's silent.

Jacob Brennan-Price (10)
St Bridget's Catholic Primary School, Warrington

Environment Poem

Our planet is cool
And the rubbish is a fool,
But the people are spoilt
Animals are dying.

Our planet is cool
And the rubbish is a fool,
With bottles, crisp packets and drinks
The sea creatures are suffering.

Our planet is cool
And the rubbish is a fool,
Something needs to be done
The litter is junk, the litter is rubbish.

Our planet is cool
And the rubbish is a fool,
Swim with glee.
In the sea.

Rebecca Grant (9)
St Bridget's Catholic Primary School, Warrington

Our Unbelievable World

Animals at the edge of extinction,
Because of the dreadful pollution,
Imagine living in that way,
In a horribly oily bay.

Animals dying every year,
Aren't you glad it doesn't happen here?
As pollution is in the air,
Some people don't even know it's there.

Danger, danger, everywhere,
Fish, ducks and beavers are there,
All dying over humans' wear,
And now, how do we fix this giant tear?

Bethany Tatlock (10)
St Bridget's Catholic Primary School, Warrington

Spoiling Our Planet

Litter, litter everywhere,
Do not drop it anywhere.

Smoke in the air gets in your hair.

Oil spills in the water,
Killing ducks.

Cars are running everywhere,
Why can't,
Why can't we share this?

More bad air gets in your hair.

Please save the planet
Everywhere.

Gavin Crane (10)
St Bridget's Catholic Primary School, Warrington

Horse

Lovely, tall, hairy and kind.
What is it?
It's a pet of mine.

Soft, fast, innocent and sweet.
What's he to you?
He's a real treat.

Clip-clop, as the feet go by
Can you hear him
Saying goodbye?

Friendly, beautiful, a powerful force.
What is it?
It's a horse!

Charlotte Connelly (11)
St John the Baptist RC Primary School, Gateshead

Football Is Great

F antastic football
O bviously the best
O f course
T he greatest sport ever
B rilliant
A s it may be
L iving the dream to become a
L egend

I magine being a
S uperstar

G ood footballers earn
R espect
E specially
A s
T ime goes on.

Liam Pine (11)
St John the Baptist RC Primary School, Gateshead

Racing Game

R ally games
A re as fast as lightning
C aution is around every turn
I ncredibly you never die
N othing ever hurts you
G o, go!

G o, go!
A gain I race
M y foot is never off the pedal until my
E ngine starts up the NOS.

Ryan Harrison (10)
St John the Baptist RC Primary School, Gateshead

My Rabbit Candy

My rabbit Candy is very, very cute,
When she was young, she was very minute.
When I got my Candy,
I was going to call her Sandy,
But the name 'Candy' jumped out,
And had a run about.
That's why I called my rabbit Candy.

Candy hops and jumps around,
And digs holes in the ground.
All day and all night,
Even when there is no light.
Her hut is canny small,
Inside there's a noisy ball.
I put her in her hut every night,
But sometimes she tries to bite,
I love my Candy, I really, really do.

Hannah Hague (11)
St John the Baptist RC Primary School, Gateshead

Dolphins

Memories flashed by . . .
The night I swam with the dolphins was amazing,
Their silver skin glistened in the moonlight,
Wherever they swam, the moon followed,
It was like a dream!

Under the water they sang a melody,
Gliding through the water at such an easy pace,
It was incredible!

My love for them reflected off the aqua sea,
'I will be back soon,' I told them,
They chattered back and then swam away with the moonlight.

Brogan McNally (11)
St John the Baptist RC Primary School, Gateshead

Senses

You have many senses
You use them every day
They are . .
Sight, hearing, touch, taste and smell.

When you're at the seaside
You can hear the children playing and laughing very loud
You can taste the wet air from the moist sand
You can smell the salty sea
You can feel the sand between your toes
You can see the waves crashing on the rocks

You have many senses
You use them every day
They are . . .
Sight, hearing, touch, taste and smell

When you're at the supermarket
You can hear the children crying and shouting, *'I want! I want!'*
You can taste the hot air floating all around
You can smell the bread being baked
You can feel the cold air as you go down the freezer aisle
You can see people packing items in bags and smiling because
it's over.

Shannon O'Neill (10)
St John the Baptist RC Primary School, Gateshead

Tigers

In the jungle
The tiger prowls
Searching silently
The creature scowls.

The furry animal
Sneaks and crawls
Hunting for prey
It bites and mauls.

Lauren Rath (10)
St John the Baptist RC Primary School, Gateshead

My Friend's Dog

My friend has a dog,
He is a boxer dog,
His name is Harry
And he is only a puppy.

He hardly ever barks,
His fur is light and dark brown,
His eyes are brown as well,
His cute puppy face is adorable.

Part of his mouth
Droops down to his chin,
But that's what makes him cute,
You could hug him all day and never let go.

He is a playful dog,
Hardly ever sad
And hardly ever bad,
He got a ball for Christmas
And plays with it 24/7.
But anyway, everybody loves him!

Bethany Codling (11)
St John the Baptist RC Primary School, Gateshead

The Blue, Blue Sea

In the blue, blue sea
There was a blue, blue ship
In the blue, blue ship
There was a blue, blue room
In the blue, blue room
There was a blue, blue cage
In the bluc, blue cage
There was a blue, blue
Squid!

Callum Reynolds (11)
St John the Baptist RC Primary School, Gateshead

Peace

Peace is a life-changing question,
That always speaks, but is never heard.
Peace can be any colour,
Whatever you imagine.
Peace tastes fresh,
Like the first day of spring.
Peace is always near,
In the rustling leaves and the clouds in the sky.
Peace is silent,
But is powerful and strong.
Peace is a friend that some people still haven't met.
Although it doesn't speak,
Peace brings love to us all.
Peace is amazing and can never be broken.

Ciara Fisher (11)
St Mary's RC Primary School, North Shields

Silence

A cool dark mist comes creeping
A resting beast, ready to pounce
A tiger's scarlet eye

Cries of wind in the silent air
Howls of dumb beasts
The tongue-less snake's hiss
Rustles of fallen trees

Growing ever larger
The fog settles the mind
A doubtful dove echoes in the dusty air

Silence.

Kirsty Jones (10)
St Mary's RC Primary School, North Shields

Hope

What is Hope?
Is she large and strong?
Is she gentle and quiet?
Is her touch soft as velvet?
Is she caring and kind
Or showy and bold?
Do her eyes glint in the moonlight?

What is Hope?
Does she sweep the world in her purple cloak,
Or is it gold, green or red?
Does she wrap around each lonely child,
Bringing it comfort and warmth?

What is Hope?
Does she dance a waltz as she flows down the street?
Does she sing as a choir of angels?
Does her voice enchant people everywhere?
Is her taste creamy or sweet?

Hope is whatever you want it to be,
A message or a song.
A dance, a friend or a hug, it's up to you to decide.

Megan Shaw (11)
St Mary's RC Primary School, North Shields

Embracing Oblivion

Death consumes your cold corpse,
By scarlet nights your soul ascends the steps
In which many more will walk,
A new beginning forming at the end,
Embrace death as it takes you,
Your hope is drowned by the fear clutching you,
Refusing to let go,
Rise up, rise up, rise up,
The time has come to meet your Creator.

Andrew Crow (11)
St Mary's RC Primary School, North Shields

The Descent

A worrying scare of . . .
The dark land of death
Old,
The deeper you think . . .
The darker the black hole will become
Darker than the night sky
It has been dead for so long
It is almost alive and walking.
The cold-hearted creature will never
Lose . . .
It will become a mystery
And then make you scream and shout . . .
Help!
Your life will end in no time!

Ashleigh Betts (11)
St Mary's RC Primary School, North Shields

Love

A golden burst of energy,
With a remaining wish,
Which is enclosed in a silver locket.

A family of joy,
Flying through a silky, smooth,
Snow-white sky.

A calm and gentle boat,
Floating on a sapphire lagoon.

A prize of affection.
A cherished treasure which will never be lost.

Catherine Woodruff (10)
St Mary's RC Primary School, North Shields

Hell Mine

It was the gates into the abyss
A tunnel full of screaming and torture
It was the black of death
No man who went in came out alive

It was Hell!

The Devil's leer with unforgivable eyes
That decimates all light
A cold-hearted breath of poison
Shatters all hope
Its silent guards waiting to take a man's soul
Into darkness and sin
These men never eat, never rest
And will never see the light of day again.

Ben Horvath (11)
St Mary's RC Primary School, North Shields

Death

Death looks like a never-ending black hole
Drowning you in blackness
Death sounds like a scream heard
Over miles and miles

Death looks like a gruesome ogre
Following you wherever you go
Death feels like a mile-long rose bush
Scratching you whenever you turn

Death tastes like a poisonous mushroom
Torturing and teasing your soul
Death reminds you of horrible things
It thrashes you until there's nothing left!

Connor Bland (10)
St Mary's RC Primary School, North Shields

Consider The Lilies . . .

Consider the rose . . .
And its beautiful petals,
The bright rosy red or the shiny pale white,
And the lovely flower-scented smell.

Consider the dolphins . . .
And their streamlined jumps,
The way they talk in their funny accent,
And their beautiful familiar personalities
Whilst swimming in the water.

Consider the dogs . . .
With long wagging tails,
And their cheerful bark,
Their beautiful soft coats.

Consider the butterflies . . .
And their colourful patterned wings,
As they softly shoot up to the sky,
Flying away.

Can Mankind make these?

Chelsea Cain (10)
St Mary's RC Primary School, North Shields

A Miner's Life

The gates of Hell were waiting for me
What evil lurks within this torture chamber?
Where do these gates lead?
What pain awaits me?
What rage will be unleashed?
What light will guide me?
The light on my helmet or the light of death?

Steven Siddle (11)
St Mary's RC Primary School, North Shields

Life - Live It To The Full

Life is a gift
It is one of the greatest gifts God has given us
In it we can find wonderful things.
But challenging things too

Life is an opportunity
To walk in the light or darkness
In life we live in hope
Until the afterlife

Life is like a river
That has an infinite journey
It can contain wonderful things
But horrible things too

Life is an adventure
That most of us accept
At the end of it we always find
What we were looking for - God

Life is everything
Everything you could ever dream of
But here's a message I advise you to take;
Love life and live it to the full.

Eleanor Conway (11)
St Mary's RC Primary School, North Shields

Christians Awake

Christians awake, the Lord has come,
Here He will make His loving kingdom.
It will be peace on Earth,
When He creates a whole new birth,
He will bring unconditional love,
Then leave His spirit and the dove.
Beyond the open doors of life,
He will stop all the strife.

Ruth Payne & Olivia Tawse (11)
St Mary's RC Primary School, North Shields

Consider The Lilies . . .

Consider the snowflake
And how it gracefully falls
Stunning in every form.
Consider the sunflower
And its petals so bright
Shining in the dark.
Consider the robin
With its red breast so soft
Delightfully singing its sweet song.
Consider the rose
With its sweet scent
Perfectly brilliant in its own way.
These marvellous things,
Is God the only Man who can make them?

Emily Chandler (10)
St Mary's RC Primary School, North Shields

God Is The . . .

God is the sun,
He shines in my heart.

God is the tree,
He gives me shade.

God is the water,
He gives me life.

God is the eye,
He gives me sight.

God is the teacher,
He gives me help.

God is the dove,
He brings peace to the world.

Keir McGovern (11)
St Mary's RC Primary School, North Shields

The Descent

The eyes of oblivion staring and drawing you closer,
an exit that will never open,
death waiting silently to take you.
The black hole sucks you in, never to be let out.
Once you are in, it is no longer silent.
It is slave-worked with pickaxes grinding,
chimneys smoking and fires burning,
trying to keep the darkness out in vain.
Industry flares and coal burns.
Only the ash escapes from Satan's pit,
this dead city with thousands of workers.
The mine stares at you, its eyes dead . . .
Now the mine is silent completely, a black lifeless void.
No one with a soul will enter now.
For in the mine still the dead workers swing the picks
and burn the coal.
They will never stop the work.

Luke Hyett (11)
St Mary's RC Primary School, North Shields

A New World Shines

The grass waves while the sun bows down at it,
The trees rustle while the birds are trying to get in,
The sky is blue, just blue, and stares there, waiting for night.
Clouds, where?
Not one in sight.
Plants waving their heads.
When night falls the stars will tinkle,
But not a sound will be heard.
The water will trickle,
But no one will hear.
The trees will rustle,
But no one hears their sound.
The grass will wave a quiet wave,
Getting ready to greet the new day.

Joel Miller (10)
St Mary's RC Primary School, North Shields

Friendship

Friendship is someone to talk to,
Friendship is someone who likes you.
It is yellow like the sun,
It is someone smiling broadly.
It is applause from a bursting crowd,
It is like two hands joining with happiness.
It is calm, peaceful, sometimes sorrowful,
But the best will always come out.

It feels soft and smooth, big and bubbly,
Small and quiet, sometimes loud.
It reminds me of my friends and family,
It is strong and powerful, full of strength.
Of course, it will never give up,
It is stronger than lightning, stronger than thunder.
Enjoy the friends you have,
Never will it die!

Sophie Nandy (9)
St Mary's RC Primary School, North Shields

Cinderella And Love

Cinderella in the night,
all dressed in sparkly white,
dazzling shoes in the bright,
how wonderful in the light,
so Cinderella said, 'Oh Prince Charming I love you so,
I am really sorry I have to go,
but Prince Charming I love you so.'
I left my shoe there on the stair,
so Prince Charming searched all the land,
so he found his lady washing up pans,
so there they did live in a beautiful land.

Khloe Mossom (9)
St Mary's RC Primary School, North Shields

Sunshine's Hope

I lie down on the dancing grass, pointing at the golden ring of sun.
As I follow the meadows beyond, I pass a lake, seeing my twin
living in its beneath; as I look up, a shining yellow strip of ribbon flows
down the middle of the water . . .

In rays of morning, I open my curtains to find the sun winking through
my window, the melody of the birds whistling in the trees,
singing the sun's lyrics.
I look at the daisies dancing to the birds' beat,
the sunflowers take command as the sun's children, as they have
always been.

As the death of the sun starts to come, I wish on a sunset's dawn
that the promises of *hope* of tomorrow will come to a new beginning, as
a new sun is born . . .

Bethany Douglas (11)
St Mary's RC Primary School, North Shields

Light

What is light?
A candle in the dark?
The sun, lighting up a darkened day?
No . . .
Light is more than that . . .
Light is peace, tranquillity and serenity
But the most precious ingredient of light is . . .
Hope!
Even a glimmer of hope is enough to destroy vast amounts of
darkness
Let us hope that one day we can join together to create not a glimmer
Of hope but vast lights that will engulf the darkness forever.

Jake Petrie (10)
St Mary's RC Primary School, North Shields

Happiness And Sadness

Sadness:

Sadness is a cold white ice ball taking over the world.
It makes me think of a horrible cold winter's day.
It sounds like someone alone, who has always been and always
will be.
It tastes like cold, bitter ice drops dropping into your mouth.
A white pool with no life in it.

Unlike,

Happiness . . .

Happiness is the opposite to sadness.
Happiness is joyful and you can have lots of fun.
The pool has life again.

Sarah C Godlington (9)
St Mary's RC Primary School, North Shields

Fear

Fear is black as darkness, like a cloud blocking the sun.
Fear is a snake hissing, tastes like a slice of raw meat.
Fear looks like a graveyard with the dead rising from their graves
And like a chicken being executed.
Fear feels like a meteor hitting the Earth with a powerful shock wave.

Mark Belshaw (10)
St Mary's RC Primary School, North Shields

Anger

Anger is red, like a burning volcano.
It sounds like a forest being destroyed.
It tastes like a red chilli pepper.
It looks like a beaming fire.
It feels harsh and hot like a demon.

James Malpas (9)
St Mary's RC Primary School, North Shields

Joy

Joy is blue, like a bluebell in the breeze
It sounds like the sea whooshing and splashing
Joy is a bluebell
Joy is like an ice cream with chocolate sauce
It tastes like sweet sugar
It feels like the sea in the Caribbean
It looks like a bluebell

Joy reminds me of the sea and sky
My favourite colour is blue,
When I think about blue it reminds me of joy.

Lauren Cummings (10)
St Mary's RC Primary School, North Shields

Anger

Anger is red like a burning fire.
It burns and hisses and sounds like a viper.
Anger tastes bitter and sour like a lemon.
It feels like rough hard sandpaper.
It reminds me of fast movement and dark places.
Anger screams and scratches like long, sharp nails running down
a blackboard.

Elizabeth Drew (10)
St Mary's RC Primary School, North Shields

Laughter

Laughter is a bluebird, tweeting in the sun,
You get tickled pink, like the icing on a bun.
It sounds like a horse's neigh, it goes on all day,
People laugh at Peter Kay, and so on, so on, so on.
Smiles are made like a house on fire,
They roll on like a car tyre.
Laughter is great. It really is.

Cally Bolam (10)
St Mary's RC Primary School, North Shields

Love

Love is a treasure, which we carry on our journey
Love is each and every one of us that makes life happy
Love is a heart waiting to be opened.
When you are bad you have love
When you are sad you have love
When you are lonely you have love.
It is with us day and night because our world is made of love.

Love is our imagination, which helps us have our pleasant dreams
Love is what helps control us from our anger
Love is our friend, but also a part of us that protects us
From the bad side.

Katie Conner (11)
St Mary's RC Primary School, North Shields

Hope

Hope is passion,
Hope is pride,
To shine on you, to shine on me.
Beam of light to make you proud,
And that's when God comes in the crowd.

Do not give up as when that happens
You've got an even worse chance to make your dream,
So that's why there are such things as hope to learn.

Liam Knight (11)
St Mary's RC Primary School, North Shields

Fear . . .

Fear is the Devil's word,
Can't run away from it,
Can't destroy it,
You have to face it
Before it'll leave you alone . . .

Thomas Wall (10)
St Mary's RC Primary School, North Shields

Emotions

Anger is red, burning, a raging fire, a bubbling cauldron, rubies and garnets, red-hot chilli peppers.

Fear's grey, hands reaching out to get you,
grey like rain clouds, rocks.

Envy is green, green like the sea, green like emeralds,
jade, leaves, grass.

Hate's purple, purple like onyx. Poison.

Sadness is black, black like night, clouding over happiness and hope,
all that's left is despair and sadness.

Hope's yellow, yellow, a light at the end of the tunnel of despair
and sadness. A candle, sweets, silver.

Happiness is, is . . . gold, all the colours of the rainbow, beautiful.
Happiness is . . . happy!

Love's bright pink, roses, strawberries, candyfloss!

Peace is pure white, ice cream, vanilla, lilies, white roses, pearls.

Francesca Ann Scanlan (10)
St Mary's RC Primary School, North Shields

Fear

Fear is purple and icy cold,
Hate is deep black and looks big and bold.
Silence is white and is very long,
It tastes of water but it doesn't pong.
Terror is fiery red, and is very scary.
If you want to avoid it, you have to be very wary.
Happiness is yellow, not bitter but sweet,
Sadness is blue, but is something you can beat.

Some of these feelings are quite bad,
But if you have too many, you might go mad!

Sean Lowery (9)
St Mary's RC Primary School, North Shields

The Four Feelings

Love is a place where anyone can go
Love is a precious thing, come on let it show

Hate is a power, stronger than all
If you stand in hate's way then you must fall

Anger is unstoppable, stay out of its way
The last one who met it died and there he lay

Happiness is the ultimate, the shining stud, the best
Happiness is my best friend, say hello, be my guest.

David Jackson (10)
St Mary's RC Primary School, North Shields

World Emotions

Terror is like a rapid roaring fire.
It's not anyone's favourite desire.

Love is a romantic feeling that runs down your spine.
Caring partners are yours and mine.

Jealousy is a wanting moan.
Something that you have to face alone.

Hope perches you at the end of your chair.
Something about which you really care.

Lynsey Hogarth (10)
St Mary's RC Primary School, North Shields

Silence

Silence is like a white floating cloud,
It sounds like a dying unicorn that dies in silence.
Silence is a daisy chain that is being made so calmly.
Silence is a soothing piece of candyfloss.
Silence is like a Third World person in hunger dying for some food
in silence!

Sam Callighan (9)
St Mary's RC Primary School, North Shields

Fear

Fear is black, black like ink,
Fear is dark, not letting you think.
Fear is hard, like a huge brick wall,
Fear is hot, overflowing us all.
Fear is the origin of all world wars,
Fear is a cat, standing up on all fours.

But peace is white, like a pure white dove,
Peace is light, like a feather from above.
Peace is white, like hard white chalk,
But peace needs to be spread, so go out and talk!

Kate Robertson (10)
St Mary's RC Primary School, North Shields

Peace

Peace is well desired for.
The hungry and the sick deserve it.
The colour is white, a plain dull colour, nothing special.
It feels cool and calm, so beautiful . . .
Peace is quiet and peaceful like the calm ocean sea.
Peace is well desired for.
The hungry and the sick deserve it.

Laura Young
St Mary's RC Primary School, North Shields

Madness

Madness is red, like uncontrollable lava
It tastes like a hyper pop, ready for work
It reminds me of a mad hospital
It sounds like a screeching owl
It looks like a hypnotised bush baby
It feels cold and icy.

Campbell Armstrong (10)
St Mary's RC Primary School, North Shields

Anger!

Anger is red like blood or a burning volcano,
It sounds like doom!
Anger is like fire at your door.
Anger tastes like hot chilli pepper.
Anger is fear, fear of doom.
Never go near or else you're doomed.
Anger is sadness, sadness for people,
All the people whose lives are ruined.
Anger looks like doom, doom, doom!
Anger is bad, bad, bad, bad!

Emily Ferguson (10)
St Mary's RC Primary School, North Shields

Anger

Anger reminds me of my mam and dad
Roaring like a volcano.
Anger is red like burning fire.
Anger tastes of a red-hot chilli pepper.
Anger sounds like an asteroid.
Anger looks like a fire burning the whole world.
It feels like a chilli.

Aidan Patterson (10)
St Mary's RC Primary School, North Shields

Happiness And Sadness

Happiness is yellow just like the sun
Sadness is blue like tears from the eye
Happiness sounds like laughter coming from a mouth
Sadness is like children crying with hunger
Happiness feels like a lovely smooth surface
Sadness feels like a melting ice cream.

Michael Atkin (10)
St Mary's RC Primary School, North Shields

Anger And Peace

Anger is like a mad rock band in your brain
But . . .
Peace is like a creamy ice cream
But . . .
Anger is red like the middle of a fire
But . . .
Peace is like a snow-white colour
But . . .
Anger sounds like an erupting volcano
But . . .
Peace sounds like a choir of angels
But . . .
Anger tastes like a red-hot chilli pepper
But . . .
Peace tastes like a white meringue
But . . .
Anger looks like a steaming, fierce storm in the dark sky
But . . .
Peace feels like you're on a marshmallow cloud
But . . .
Anger feels hot and spicy.

Roddy Weir (9)
St Mary's RC Primary School, North Shields

Death

Death is dark and black like a bat,
but is not lucky like a black cat.
Death is like bitter herbs that whip
your tongue or sour like a lemon.
It is a flower, all shrivelled up
and dead lying on the grass.
It feels like nails down a blackboard,
scraping and screeching.
Death sounds like a gunshot or a baby crying.
Death is a hole in your heart.

Megan Storey (10)
St Mary's RC Primary School, North Shields

Jealousy Is . . . ?

Jealousy is as green as an emerald,
It sparkles all day,
It doesn't leave you alone.

Jealousy is a simple desire,
You need something,
You need to keep it.

Jealousy is a shout out loud,
'Get something else,'
But you want a certain possession.

Jealousy sounds like thunder,
Roaring around you,
It just won't go.

Jealousy tastes a bit like sweetcorn,
Sometimes it is chewy.
It gets stuck in your teeth.

But jealousy goes away.
It is not permanent.
It is not that bad . . . is it . . . ?

Megan Clery (10)
St Mary's RC Primary School, North Shields

War Leads To Peace

War is a camouflaged tank, firing its shells.
War is the infantry firing the deafening rifles.
War is aircraft getting shot from the skies.
War is ships sinking in the deep blue seas.
War is death like scattered bodies of men.

Peace is white like a flying dove.
Peace is pink like strawberry ice cream.
Peace is another country understanding their ways.
Peace is life with humans.

Callum Rogers (9)
St Mary's RC Primary School, North Shields

Love

Love is pink like a big pink heart.
Love sounds like soft music that will never part.
Love tastes like ice cream melting in the sun.
Love looks like children having great fun.
Heartbreak and love is always rife,
So make the best of our fabulous life.

Love must remind us of hope and faith.
Love must never remind you of darkness and death.
Love feels like a pink cloud of candyfloss,
Always floating and acting like a boss.
But love can be as hard as chalk,
So go around again and let people talk again.

Elizabeth O'Neill (9)
St Mary's RC Primary School, North Shields

Cross Road

Anger is red, as red as blood
Anger is dangerous, just like a monster
Snapping its tongue
It's as rough as a dinosaur's back.
Cry your last word, as you're about to die.
It feels as painful as a train crashing into you,
Ripping you up bit by bit into tiny pieces

Unlike peace,
Peace is blue,
It sounds like the ocean sweeping the sand away,
It tastes like fresh water running down your throat,
It is as smooth as a crystal gleaming in your face.

Rianna Alves Cowey (9)
St Mary's RC Primary School, North Shields

The Descent

The very gates of Hell have just opened to you
and it will always wait for you.
If you go near it you will shout for help
and you will get lost so it's up to you.
Have you ever been anywhere silent?
Well here is a place now that you haven't even dreamt of.
If anyone dare go there evil rules it,
you may go through the entrance but what about the exit?
There is no exit, it is all black, so if you enter you will come out,
but not alive, that is the end of you, that is the end of the world.

Poroushat Farokhzad (10)
St Mary's RC Primary School, North Shields

The Descent

The Devil's stronghold.
It is the eyes of oblivion,
The gateway to the dark abyss which no candle can save
For ice is hotter and the night is brighter than the Devil's leer.
There is no light on the other side,
But only a forgotten black-robed bone man
Wielding a scythe and a blood-red devil king with a crooked smile.
This is not a mine, it is a black portal to Hell's biggest torture chamber
Which is dark enough to make a heart a black lump of coal
And turn a human to a devil, a skeleton or a reaper of souls.

William Hayward (11)
St Mary's RC Primary School, North Shields

Anger

Anger is red, like a fierce fire.
Anger is bitter, like an ice cube dropping in your mouth.
Anger is loud, like a crackling fire.
Anger is destructive, like a bomb about to go off.
Anger is oozing, like a volcano's lava.

Jack Robert Hetherington (9)
St Mary's RC Primary School, North Shields

What Is Life?

Life is peaceful,
Life is enjoyment,
No matter what you are and who,
You will still be remembered

God is with you, surrounding you,
No space to move at all.
He has left you alone by yourself,
Just yourself, to make your own decisions.

Pride and courage are in your life.
Life is the most valuable part of you,
No one can buy it at all,
Not even if you do it for yourself.

Life is everything!

Jonathan Whyte (11)
St Mary's RC Primary School, North Shields

Mixed Emotions

Fear is dark blue
Something that you can't control
Like the crashing of the sea

But peace is white and pure
And when you're in it it's a really good cure
It feels like Heaven
All fresh and dreamy
It tastes so white and creamy
It's something that's so surreal.

Elizabeth Cartwright (10)
St Mary's RC Primary School, North Shields

The Anger And The Peace!

Anger is red like a volcano bursting out
with fire and smoke spreading across the city.
Anger sounds like a hissing snake
with a crackling tongue in the distance.
Anger tastes spicy like a red-hot chilli pepper.
It feels hot when it starts and cold when it ends.

Unlike peace.
Peace is gentle like a fluffy bunny.
It feels smooth like marble ice.
Peace looks creamy like a dream, so dreamy.

Abigail Lemberger (10)
St Mary's RC Primary School, North Shields

Winter's Night

It was a cold winter's night and the snow was hugging the ground.
The wind was howling all day.
The leaves were chittering and chattering.
The moon was walking across the sky and the sun was yawning.
The snowdrops were piling on top of each other and all was quiet.

Ben Fitton (11)
St Stephen's CE Primary School, Audenshaw

Tiger

T eeth as sharp as razors
I s as deadly as a loaded gun
G reat powerful creature
E nemies will cower
R avenous for blood.

Jack Johnson (11)
St Stephen's CE Primary School, Audenshaw

In The Zoo

It was dark and windy in the zoo that night,
Night sky was silver and the stars twinkled,
Time went by like a click of my fingers,
Hippos were sleeping as they went through their dreams,
Elephants slept ready for the next lovely day,
Zebras were laid away awake as they were waiting for tomorrow,
Out in the open the sun rose,
Ostriches awoke also all the rest of the animals
All ready for the start of the lovely sunny day.

Bethany Ashmore (11)
St Stephen's CE Primary School, Audenshaw

Maggot, Worm Or Caster

Maggot, worm or caster,
Which do fish eat faster?
A tug on the rod,
Pop! The float goes under,
Then my heart starts to beat like thunder,
But still I wonder,
Which do fish eat faster?
Maggot, worm or caster.

Thomas Peake-Lees (11)
St Stephen's CE Primary School, Audenshaw

My Anger Poem

Anger sounds like an erupting volcano,
Anger feels like a punch in the belly,
Anger is the smell of burnt toast,
Anger tastes like scalding hot lava,
Anger is my reminder of the Devil,
Anger is the look of Hell.

Conor Hand (11)
St Stephen's CE Primary School, Audenshaw

Sadness

Sadness is the colour blue like wet flowing tears,
Of scary dreams and worrying fears,
Sadness is the sign of loss or broken love,
When no tears are shed it is a sign of a memory breaking through,
Or a happy soul with no worries,
Tears are salty like shores of the sea
And painful like a bite of a shark.
Every time someone cries a wave is added to the sea.
Every time someone smiles the sun steals the waves.

Samantha Derbyshire (11)
St Stephen's CE Primary School, Audenshaw

Fun

Fun is multicoloured like a rainbow shining,
Fun sounds like someone laughing,
Fun feels like someone skipping and playing,
Fun tastes like an ice cream melting in my mouth,
Fun looks like someone enjoying themselves,
Fun reminds me of children playing on a sunny beach,
Fun smells like children getting presents.

Yasmin Garratt (11)
St Stephen's CE Primary School, Audenshaw

Love

Love is red.
Love feels like butterflies in your belly.
Love looks like two people kissing.
Love reminds you of two people hugging.
Love smells like chocolate.
Love tastes like marshmallows.

Levi Blackburn (10)
St Stephen's CE Primary School, Audenshaw

The Lonely Kirks

As day grows old and night takes over,
Light passes over the last clover,
The shadows eat away the prominent light
That puts life into the lonely kirks.
The sweltering heat slowly disappears
As a cold breeze creeps into the lonely night,
The moon appears high in the sky
And the trees' shadows;
Alone they lie.
The people passing by think about
Anything that springs to mind,
But not one thinks of the lonely kirks
That stand lonely forever.

Adam Freeburn (11)
St Stephen's CE Primary School, Audenshaw

Storm

Thunder, thunder, oh I wonder,
Where electricity comes from,
But when lightning strikes,
A bright light hikes
And hits a high kite,
Floating in the lonely night,
When the rain comes down,
In the silent town,
The weather vane puts up a fight,
To save the church against the thunderous light,
Thunder, thunder, oh I still wonder,
Where electricity comes from.

Jordan Heathcote (11)
St Stephen's CE Primary School, Audenshaw

Darkness

Darkness reminds me of blackness everywhere,
I'm trapped in it and I can't get out.
It smells like dirt that I can't get rid of.
It tastes like fog creeping up on me,
Its haunted feeling makes me want to scream.
Darkness is like a dead forest with no trees growing,
Everything is dead.
The wind whispers, 'Go away, save yourself'
And each time it is said, the voice grows louder.
Darkness feels like I'm stumbling everywhere I step.

Saariah Qureshi (11)
St Stephen's CE Primary School, Audenshaw

Fear

Fear is black like the dead of night.
Fear looks like your worst nightmare.
Fear tastes like rancid food.
Fear sounds like a scream of death.
Fear reminds me of a knife going through my heart.
Fear feels like a pack of wolves stalking me.
Fear smells like a burning deadly fire.

Joshua Katihrob (10)
St Stephen's CE Primary School, Audenshaw

Darkness

Darkness is the colour black
Like a night sky with no stars.
Darkness sounds like the loudest thunderclap.
Darkness tastes like evil.
Darkness smells like smoke rising in the air.
Darkness reminds me of a mad professor.

Cayla Morris (10)
St Stephen's CE Primary School, Audenshaw

Silence

Silence is white like the soft fluffy clouds that float in the sky.
Silence smells like the buzzing bees that collect pollen from the flowers.
Silence looks like my budgie falling asleep on my fleece.
Silence tastes like I am just cutting into a lovely steaming hot roast dinner.
Silence sounds like a cool breeze softly flowing past you.
Silence feels like my budgie's soft feathery belly on my fingers.

Emma Price (11)
St Stephen's CE Primary School, Audenshaw

Fear

Fear is black like the darkness of the night.
Fear tastes like the rust off steal.
Fear sounds like a moaning devil in your head.
Fear reminds you of a ghost roaming the empty streets.
Fear looks like a bath full of your own blood.
Fear smells like fire burning your house to the ground.
Fear feels like a best friend ripping your heart out.

Thomas Paddon (10)
St Stephen's CE Primary School, Audenshaw

Anger

Anger is the colour of a flame burning from house to house.
Anger tastes like a very hot chilli bubbling in your mouth.
Anger looks like lava bursting out of a volcano.
Anger reminds me of fire burning.
Anger sounds like fireworks exploding.
Anger smells like spices and smoke.
Anger feels like a punch in the face.

Zakee Siddique
St Stephen's CE Primary School, Audenshaw

The Dark Night Poem

It was a dark freezing night,
The sea was very quiet whispering to the cliffs.
The grass was shivering with fear,
Arguing with the crunchy leaves as they broke.

The houses hesitated as they got frostbite.
The slide was so cold it slid into a puddle.
The cupboard however was cosy in a blanket huddle.

Then it got sunny,
The trees stroked the bunny,
The lazy sea laid back and relaxed.

Sagar Arjan (11)
St Stephen's CE Primary School, Audenshaw

Love

Love is as pink as a dainty rose,
Love looks like a heart shaded in red,
Love smells like lovely fresh new roses,
Love tastes like creamy chocolate saved for you,
Love sounds like music that just flicks on,
Love feels like you're a part of life properly,
Love reminds you of fireworks being set off across your house.

Victoria Warburton (11)
St Stephen's CE Primary School, Audenshaw

Love

Love is like a sparkling diamond,
Love is like a piece of rich chocolate,
Love is like a very first kiss,
Love is like a person running miles and miles for him,
Love is like a new heart, eager for love.

Katie Wellens (11)
St Stephen's CE Primary School, Audenshaw

Darkness

Darkness is black like a wolf roaming the streets at night.
It sounds like a scream piercing the silence.
It tastes like swamp water that has had lots of strange things in.
It smells like rotting floorboards which have gone uncleaned
for centuries.
It looks like the outline of a stranger in the distance.
It feels like a bony hand creeping across your shoulder.
It reminds me of sitting in a room for hours on end with no one
to talk to.

Paul Hannon (11)
Sacred Heart RC Primary School, Newcastle-upon-Tyne

Jealousy

Jealousy is dark green
It sounds like people shouting over nothing
It smells like salty water in your mouth
It smells like wood burning in a bonfire
It looks like volcanoes exploding
It feels like sick swirling in the pit of your tummy
It reminds me of how I see friends breaking up and
never being friends again.

Tonisha Witherspoon (11)
Sacred Heart RC Primary School, Newcastle-upon-Tyne

Love

Love is red like a loving heart.
It sounds like two birds tweeting in the garden.
It tastes like melted chocolate in your mouth.
It smells like a rose growing in your garden.
It looks like an apple falling from a tree.
It feels like a dolphin swimming back and forth.
It reminds me of my family and friends.

Lauren Brown (11)
Sacred Heart RC Primary School, Newcastle-upon-Tyne

Hunger

Hunger is orange like the top of a burger bun.
It sounds like people crying in other countries for more food.
It tastes like melted chocolate dipped with marshmallows.
It smells like a food factory bringing out a new sponge cake.
It looks like a fast food palace in the centre of town.
It feels like a burnt burger in a bread roll.
It reminds me of going to the KFC for the first time with my dad.

Henry Chamberlain (10)
Sacred Heart RC Primary School, Newcastle-upon-Tyne

Fear

Fear is cream like an icy, pale face.
It sounds like rain crashing down in a back alley.
It tastes like raw pasta which crunches in your wet mouth.
It smells like cold air rushing up your nostrils.
It looks like an isolated boy sitting in an empty street.
It feels like loneliness and pain of someone scared.
It reminds me of an everlasting pit of darkness which waits at
the end of your life.

Euan Graham (11)
Sacred Heart RC Primary School, Newcastle-upon-Tyne

Darkness

Darkness is black like a big black hole.
It sounds like thunder banging in a storm.
It tastes like tons of lava in you stomach.
It smells like burning fire.
It looks like a surd dripping with blood.
It feels like being struck by lightning.
It reminds me of the murders in our city.

Richy Rowley (11)
Sacred Heart RC Primary School, Newcastle-upon-Tyne

Love

Love is a deep scarlet like a rose.
It sounds like a lullaby in a child's bedroom.
It tastes like pink fluffy marshmallows dipped in melted,
creamy, warm milk chocolate.
It smells like fresh lavender, picked from a garden.
It looks like a box of Turkish delights in red wrapping and in
the shape of hearts.
It feels like a velvet blanket wrapped around a baby.
It reminds me of a tulip growing in the summer sun.

Katy Seymour (11)
Sacred Heart RC Primary School, Newcastle-upon-Tyne

Love

Love is pink like a growing rose.
It sounds like two lovebirds tweeting a love song.
It tastes like marshmallows sitting peacefully on top of some
hot chocolate.
It smells like a freshly baked cake ready to be eaten.
It looks like colourful feathers on a bird.
It feels like silk being wrapped around you.
It reminds me of a newborn baby silently sleeping in her
mother's arms.

Daisy Thornton (10)
Sacred Heart RC Primary School, Newcastle-upon-Tyne

Love

Love is pink like a rose petal.
It sounds like calm music playing.
It tastes like strawberries dipped in chocolate.
It looks like a beautiful view from the Eiffel Tower.
It feels like two poodles licking you.
It reminds me of my family and how much they love me.

Kirstie Storey (11)
Sacred Heart RC Primary School, Newcastle-upon-Tyne

Anger

Anger is orange and red like a fire ablaze.
It sounds like a deathly hot pan of a witch's cauldron bubbling
over a stove.
It tastes like lava entering the sight of your tongue in fear.
It smells like tobacco burning, surrounding you, coughing,
feeling scared.
It looks like a dungeon, haunted in darkness.
It feels like an old fingerprint, the owner unknown.
It reminds me of a ghostly image, screaming in my left ear
like a baby.

Alice Poynter (11)
Sacred Heart RC Primary School, Newcastle-upon-Tyne

Fun

Fun is blue like a blue sky.
Fun sounds like being out of breath when you are having a good time.
Fun smells like freshly cut grass on a hot summer day.
Fun tastes like ice cream with monkey blood and a flake.
Fun feels like happiness and it is a very good feeling.
Fun looks like friends smiling and playing.
Fun reminds me of playing football, tennis and running.

Jacques Armstrong (11)
Sacred Heart RC Primary School, Newcastle-upon-Tyne

Silence

Silence is grey like a looming stormcloud roaming across the sky.
It sounds like a pebble falling swiftly downwards.
It tastes like porridge, cold and thick, slowly being churned inside
the mouth.
It looks like a motionless silhouette, light eerily shining all around it.
It feels like a draught of icy air swooping through the room.
It reminds me of the tension between people.

Rachel Hardy (11)
Sacred Heart RC Primary School, Newcastle-upon-Tyne

Darkness

Darkness is like a dark black shadow beneath the broken street light
It sounds like scary loud noises in the middle of the night
It tastes like stale ale which has been in the cellar for years
It smells like old, damp, musty books
It looks like a ghostly person lingering under a lamp post
It feels like a deadly image of an axe being thrown towards you
It reminds me of a murderer running through the streets at night.

Liam Colligan (10)
Sacred Heart RC Primary School, Newcastle-upon-Tyne

Love

Love is pink like a soft marshmallow.
It sounds like birds tweeting in the trees.
It tastes like candyfloss.
It smells like roses from a flower garden.
It looks like rose petals falling from the light blue sky.
It feels like a soft fluffy pillow.
It reminds me of the good times I have with my friends and family.

Hannah Louise McKenna (11)
Sacred Heart RC Primary School, Newcastle-upon-Tyne

Love

Love is light pink like a big love heart.
It sounds like the laughter of children.
It tastes like warm chocolate, melting in your mouth.
It smells like a bright red rose in the summer.
It looks like a love heart which is filled with happiness.
It feels like warm arms wrapped around you.
It reminds me of the one I love.

Molly Hands (11)
Sacred Heart RC Primary School, Newcastle-upon-Tyne

Jealousy

Jealousy is green like radioactive acid.
It sounds like somebody else having fun with something you
don't have.
It tastes like anger.
It smells like the scent of chilli peppers.
It looks like a pool of green liquid.
It feels like a lump of jelly in your hand.
It reminds me of somebody showing off.

William Reynolds (11)
Sacred Heart RC Primary School, Newcastle-upon-Tyne

Darkness

Darkness is black like an endless tunnel.
It has no sound, just pure deathly silence.
It has a dull taste, like water, left in a bottle for months.
It smells like damp soil, left in a confined space.
It looks like a dark demon, rising up to engulf your mind and soul.
It feels like swimming in a cold grey sea and being dragged under
the surface.
It reminds me of losing a friend and not knowing what to do.

Catherine Heads (11)
Sacred Heart RC Primary School, Newcastle-upon-Tyne

Fear

Fear is blue like the early night sky.
It sounds like a woman screaming in pain.
It tastes like disgusting meat from millenniums ago.
It smells like an old deserted cellar.
It looks like an old watered down river.
It feels like a body rotting away.
It reminds me of when everyone has deserted me.

Conor Wall (11)
Sacred Heart RC Primary School, Newcastle-upon-Tyne

Darkness

Darkness is black like a deathly tarantula creeping up your back
at midnight.
It sounds like a wolf howling in the moonlit sky.
It tastes like sewer water which has been left in a drain for hundreds
of years.
It smells like burning wood with smoke bursting out to enter
your nose.
It looks like an eagle swooping in the dark sky just about to catch
its prey inside its mouth.
It feels like a snake slithering down your bony spine.
It reminds me of a deadly image of a wolf howling in the
moonlit sky.

Thomas Gains (10)
Sacred Heart RC Primary School, Newcastle-upon-Tyne

Silence

Silence is black like a midnight sky with a beam of moonlight
It sounds like footsteps and owls hooting loudly through a forest
of oak
It tastes like cold winter air upon the tip of your tongue
It smells like dust and old red wine left in the cellar for years
It looks like a vacant and dark room, cobwebs and a black hole in
the middle of it
It feels like a ghostly image, uncertain to speak and that the shadow
That's been creeping up on you for the last few years is one of
your lost loved ones
It reminds me of a wounded child, left lonely to die.

Tom Howley (10)
Sacred Heart RC Primary School, Newcastle-upon-Tyne

Hate

Hate is red like a raging fire burning through the dead woods.
It sounds like an exploding grenade during battle.
It tastes like sizzling chillies burning your mouth.
It smells like the thick layer of smoke from a burning forest.
It looks like an evil smirk from some ferocious beast.
It feels like the edge of a knife piercing your heart.
It reminds me of a plane crashing into an uninhabited area of
the world.

Sam Gilbride (11)
Sacred Heart RC Primary School, Newcastle-upon-Tyne

Love

Love is pink like a heart.
It sounds like two birds tweeting a soft melody.
It tastes like a hot Sunday dinner.
It smells like the countryside grass on a hot summer's day.
It looks like the view on top of a mountain.
It feels like a marshmallow in your mouth melting.
It reminds me of my family and loved ones.

Shannon Gains (11)
Sacred Heart RC Primary School, Newcastle-upon-Tyne

Fear

Fear is red like blood pouring from your soul.
It sounds like a penetrating scream ripping through you.
It tastes like rotten vile meat that has been left for centuries.
It smells like rotten blue cheese.
It looks like an angry bull charging towards you.
It feels like a thousand fists digging into your stomach.
It reminds me of death.

Paul Wiper (11)
Sacred Heart RC Primary School, Newcastle-upon-Tyne

Hate

Hate is crimson like a blood-stained sword, constantly lashing out.
It sounds like a drilling headache.
It tastes like a cup of bitter liquid.
It smells like rotten, acrid debris.
It looks like a looming castle, forbidding entry.
It feels like a bite of a venomous cobra.
It reminds me of a time of sadness and loneliness.

Amar Mohammed (11)
Sacred Heart RC Primary School, Newcastle-upon-Tyne

Fun

Fun is yellow like a sun shining in the sky
It sounds like excitement coming from day and night
It tastes like roses coming from everywhere
It smells like laughter coming from the air
It looks like everyone is playing and enjoying themselves
It feels like air coming with a present every day and night
It reminds me of playing around and enjoying myself.

Noor-Ul Sabah (10)
Sacred Heart RC Primary School, Newcastle-upon-Tyne

Love

Love is pink like a fluffy marshmallow
It sounds like birds high up in the sky chirping
It tastes like ice cream covered in hot melted chocolate
It smells like roses in a neatly cut garden
It looks like roses being lit up by the shining sun
It feels like extra soft silk
It reminds me of getting presents from my mam and dad.

Amber Cothill (10)
Sacred Heart RC Primary School, Newcastle-upon-Tyne

Before The Hunt

Calming owls
calm me,
swooping vines
hear me,
shining stars
guide me,
chirping birds
guide my way through this journey.
As the moon protects the little stars
so may I escape the king of the jungle,
as the lion stalks his prey.
So may I first to spy my prey.
Chirping birds hear me,
smiling clouds steal my heart.
Teasing animals laugh with me,
lead me to my hunt.

Ellie Flaherty McConnell (9)
Spring Gardens Primary School, North Shields

Before The Hunt

Whistling wind
blow me.
Hooting owls
calm me.
Shooting waterfall
light me.
Crashing thunder
protect me,
show me my way to my prey.
May I escape the gloom and lonely moon
as these little creatures tremble.
As the fancy breeze
gently softens against my face please . . .
lead me to my hunt.

Bethany Brice (9)
Spring Gardens Primary School, North Shields

Before The Hunt

Calming birds,
calm me,
dancing vines,
defend me,
shining leaves,
shimmer me,
echoing owls,
show me the way through my journey.
As the rustling trees protect the animals,
so may I be as quiet as a mouse.
As the lion tiptoes up to its prey,
so may I escape the beasts in this living forest.
Living forest hear me,
cooling trees blow me,
teasing shadows smile with me.
Lead me to my hunt.

Robyn Smith (9)
Spring Gardens Primary School, North Shields

The Leaf

A leaf ambles
across the streets.
Blows round a
lamp post that shimmers.
It crawls in front of
a house like a burglar.
Leaf shouts, 'Stop it wind!'
Hopes the wind will die.
Swoops across the road
As it overhears the wind go.
It stays in the same spot.
Wind flies back.
leaf tries to escape
swaying side to side.

Jack Miller (11)
Spring Gardens Primary School, North Shields

Before The Hunt

Howling wind,
calm me,
waving trees,
cool me,
sparkling moon,
help me,
cheeping birds,
guide me,
through the awful traps of the forest.
As the trees protect
the lonely birds,
so may I escape
the ravenous beast.
As the beast stalks its prey
so may I be first to spy my game.
Living forest hail me.
Teasing trees follow me.
Whistling wind smile with me.
Lead me to my hunt.

Peter Dyers (9)
Spring Gardens Primary School, North Shields

Winter Woodland

Woodland leaves whisper
trees whistle
snowdrops shiver
foxes chase
rabbits run.
Dark nights whirl
they approach quickly
hiding everything in their path
winter comes at last!

Emily Johnston (10)
Spring Gardens Primary School, North Shields

Before The Hunt

Crashing waterfalls,
cool me,
shrieking birds,
hear me,
waving trees,
guide me,
frightening thunder,
hide me,
hooting owls,
calm me,
shooting stars,
shine on me,
glittering moon,
hail me,
shining river,
lead me to my hunt.

Lauren Agnew (9)
Spring Gardens Primary School, North Shields

As The Kitchen Slowly Warms Up

As the kitchen slowly warms up
The bright light is switched on.
It jumps and jives,
The cooker is turned on.
It lets out a big friendly grin,
Cupboard doors begin to dance.
Fridge begins to shiver,
The freezer's teeth start to chatter,
Toaster begins to mumble and grumble.
About the day ahead,
The plughole soundly gurgles . . .
The gale outside whirls, the windows open,
The icy wind blows in.

Emily Morison (11)
Spring Gardens Primary School, North Shields

Before The Hunt

Singing crickets,
charm me,
sparkling stars,
lead me,
gleaming moon,
soothe me,
weeping birds
calm me,
through the wilderness,
as the monkeys chat to the trees,
so may I escape the beasts
in this lonely forest.
As the cats stalk their prey
so may I be first to spy my game.
Lonely forest hear me,
soothing wind still my heart,
chattering monkeys smile with me.
Lead me to my hunt.

Jordan Greener (9)
Spring Gardens Primary School, North Shields

Giggling Diaries

My diary giggles
Reading secrets.
The pages whisper to each other
Spreading gossip.
My pen spits ink.
The key grins
As the lock is forced to open.

When I try to read my secrets
The diary defiantly flicks the pages
And my diary cover smirks.

Jade Abraham (11)
Spring Gardens Primary School, North Shields

Before The Hunt

Tweeting birds,
calm me,
booming thunder,
hear me,
rustling leaves,
cool me,
crashing waterfalls,
guide my way through the forest.
As the moon protects the lonely trees
so may I escape the vines
in this living forest.
As the lion tears at meat
so may I be first to go on my journey.
Snapping twigs hear me,
chilling river still my heart.
Lead me to my hunt.

Joe Browell (8)
Spring Gardens Primary School, North Shields

Before The Hunt

Singing birds,
calm me,
fluttering butterflies
guide me,
clashing waterfalls
cool me,
shining waters
light my way through this overgrown garden.
As the twisting vines protect the lonely trees
so may I be first to discover the jungle traps.
Scratching monkeys hail me
falling leaves play with me
hooting owls do your lovely tune.
Lead me to my hunt.

Amy Tennant (9)
Spring Gardens Primary School, North Shields

Before The Hunt

Calming wind,
calm me,
sparkling rain,
cool me,
glistening stars,
guide me,
roaring lion,
defend me on my tour through the bush,
as the creatures protect the insects
so may I get through the bush in one piece.
Whistling waterfalls,
hail me,
waving trees,
smile with me,
living shadows,
hear me.
Lead me to my hunt.

Jessica Hull (9)
Spring Gardens Primary School, North Shields

Before The Hunt

Rolling oceans,
cool me,
moving trees,
hide me,
crashing rocks,
protect me,
lurking shadows,
block the moonlight
from my face.
As the waters provide the fish,
may this forest provide my prey.
Inviting caves, shelter my head,
fine soil, soften my path.
Lead me to my hunt.

Jean-Luke Minchella (9)
Spring Gardens Primary School, North Shields

Before The Hunt

Shimmering stars,
hear me,
hooting owls,
hail me,
growling tigers,
help me,
shooting stars,
guide me,
booming thunder,
protect me on my journey.
As the trees
hide the animals
so may I escape
the snares
in this living forest.
So may I spy my game.
Lead me to my hunt.

Lauren Rootes (9)
Spring Gardens Primary School, North Shields

Before The Hunt

Splashing rain,
cool me,
tweeting birds,
hear me,
crunching leaves,
calm me,
shining stars,
shine on me,
as I go into the forest.
Booming thunder,
protect me,
teasing monkeys,
smile with me,
lead me to my hunt.

Thomas Fletcher (8)
Spring Gardens Primary School, North Shields

In The Dark Streets

In the dark streets
On a dark night
A mist comes in.
Lamp posts struggling to
Shine on the cracked dirty path
The heavy blanket makes seeing tricky.
Lamp posts endeavour to make it brighter
Wink, wink!

Jack Bennett (11)
Spring Gardens Primary School, North Shields

The River Of Thunder

The thunder is like fire
It is a white frightening river striking from the sky
As frightening as a ghost
5,000 bolts!

Jack Lillico (10)
Spring Gardens Primary School, North Shields

Sunset

As peaceful as an empty room
as beautiful as a shooting star
the darkening purple sky
a ball of fire
as hot as an oven
it is a purple coin slowly fading away.

Kirsty Rudd
Spring Gardens Primary School, North Shields

Boulders

B ig boulders killing everything in front of them.
O ld ones and young ones, waiting to strike!
U nknown when they'll fall.
L urking on the mountains about to fall.
D on't go in front of a boulder.
E very move could make one fall!
R acing down the hilltops -
S plat!

Adam Dranfield (9)
Taxal & Fernilee CE Primary School, High Peak

Cheese

C rumbling in my mouth,
H ave some tasty cheese,
E nergy you will get,
E at it, it's tasty,
S avoury it is!
E at cheese, it's lovely!

Ben Stones (9)
Taxal & Fernilee CE Primary School, High Peak

Earth In Space

E arth is a planet,
A planet on which we live,
R ed planet near the sun,
T he sun is a ball of fire,
H ot, hot sun!

Alice Platt (9)
Taxal & Fernilee CE Primary School, High Peak

Bees

There are all kinds of bees . . .
Army bees
And mardy bees
Mean bees
And clean bees
Sporty bees
And naughty bees
Yellow bees
And black bees
Tall bees, small bees
Fatty bees
And tatty bees
'Shoo' these bees please!
Kind bees
And blind bees
Baby bees
And lady bees
Happy bees
And nappy bees . . .
And . . .
That's it!

Edward Austin (8)
Taxal & Fernilee CE Primary School, High Peak

The Pirate's Boat

A shiny new boat!
Help, I'm drowning!
Oh no, the treasure's fallen into the sea!
Yikes! We're heading for the rocks!
Yippee, we've made it to shore,
But next time, I'm driving!

Joshua Lomas (9)
Taxal & Fernilee CE Primary School, High Peak

Rainbow

Red is like blood dripping out of the tap,
Red is like a diamond in a very special delicate box,
Red is a beautiful colour.
Yellow is as shiny as the sun,
Yellow is as yellow as a sunflower,
Yellow is a beautiful colour.
Pink is as pink as a rose,
Pink is as bright as a very pink face.
Green is as shiny as a field of grass,
Green is as tall as a tree.
Orange is a very big jug of orange juice,
Orange is as tasty as an orange.
Purple is as gooey as purple goo all over the house.
Blue is as bright as the sky.

Amy Jodrell (9)
Taxal & Fernilee CE Primary School, High Peak

Train

T wo sides of the train look pretty
R ailway's so clean
A ll trains are fast
I n you go
N ice trip wasn't it!

Adam Fox (9)
Taxal & Fernilee CE Primary School, High Peak

Cars

C ars are roaring non-stop like the Bugatti Veyron
A steering wheel can turn very tight
R acing cars go around the corners
S peeding across the finish line.

Elliot Whelan (9)
Taxal & Fernilee CE Primary School, High Peak

Bubbles

The bubbles pop more and more,
as they reach the bathroom floor.
The smell is like a white dove,
and that's the smell I just love.
The bubbles are like a light blue sky,
but with the clouds floating by.

As I see them popping away,
I can see them creating more bubbles far and away.
Day and night I take a bath,
there I sit, having a laugh.
As I step into the bubbly bath,
there they are, gleaming away like a white diamond.

Cracking as I pass, it makes me feel excited,
the warmth of the water makes them shine,
it is like a miracle that has just passed by.

Laura Alexander (11)
Teesside Preparatory & High School, Stockton-on-Tees

Holiday

I went on holiday yesterday
I went to a magical place.

Someone special lives there
Try and guess who
If you can't I'll give you a clue.

He's got a white beard
He wears red clothes
He gives you presents once a year
Try and guess who
If you can't I'll give you a clue.

He's quite fat
You leave him milk and cookies at night
Try and guess who
It is Santa from the North Pole.

Brogan Kerr (8)
Teesside Preparatory & High School, Stockton-on-Tees

Castles

Some castles are haunted
Haunted castles are creepy
In the night they are scary
All haunted castles are creaky.

Some castles are fairy tale
Fairy tale castles are filled with jewels, all glittering
They dazzle in the gleaming light
Inside there are fairies fluttering.

Some castles are wacky
They always look strange
Some are even bouncy
When I come out I'm never sane.

This is the last type of castle
A royal castle
They are always grand
Just like a fairy tale castle they dazzle.

Annie Chin (9)
Teesside Preparatory & High School, Stockton-on-Tees

I Like . . .

I like the sun, I like the clouds,
I like everything around,
The sky, the air, sounds and places.
I like everything there is,
Especially flowers blowing in the sun,
Swaying and waving, what fun.
Daisies and roses, lavender and trees,
I like everything, also the breeze.

Alexandra Drysdale (8)
Teesside Preparatory & High School, Stockton-on-Tees

Identity

I have two dogs
They love to play with frogs
I love riding horses
As they go clipperty-clop

I like to splash in puddles
And give my parents cuddles
My mum and dad are proud of me
And I am as happy as can be!

I am seven years old and like to swim
That is my best thing!

My parents think that I am kind
My friend thinks I am fine!
My pet thinks I am generous
I think I am special!

Emily Bullock (8)
Teesside Preparatory & High School, Stockton-on-Tees

Daisy

Daisy, Daisy yellow and white
You shimmer and shimmer in my sight
All day long you sit and shine
Oh I wish I could pick you so you could be mine.

You are swaying in the breeze
Your pollen collected by all the bees
Your petals colourful and bright
All through the forest and all through the night.

Daisy, Daisy you're so beautiful
Oh such a pretty sight
Always smiling when I see you
I know you love me and I love you too!

Emma White (11)
Teesside Preparatory & High School, Stockton-on-Tees

Castles

I wish I was in a fairy tale castle
With magical things that will happen
Gold and silver glittering brightly
Little fairies fluttering lightly.

I wish I was in a haunted castle
With ghosts and ghouls and chains that rattle
The spooky feeling grips my might
I wonder if anything bites.

I wish I was in a grand castle
With a royal theme fit for a princess
Red and crimson, nice and soft
It's got to be bold with some spots.

I wish I was in the grand castle with a beautiful comfy throne
I wish I was in the haunted castle with all the spooky ghosts
I wish I was in the fairy tale castle with the fairies fluttering wings
But all the castles are special to me.

Georgia Yawson (8)
Teesside Preparatory & High School, Stockton-on-Tees

Fireworks

Fireworks zooming from Earth out into space
We look at them and think, *wow*
What an amazing chase.
Meanwhile sparklers glitter in the moonlight
People watch the fireworks as they glow
Some of them look just like snow.
We hear them fizz and bang,
Sometimes I see them fall
In colours so elegant and loud
Jumping and pouncing down through the place
So beautiful to cheer the human race.

Lilly Connolly (7)
Teesside Preparatory & High School, Stockton-on-Tees

Rose

Soft and red, your petals gleam
under a single moonlit beam.
In the wind your leaves sway
glowing softly day by day.

You are the flowers' queen
kind and gentle, not horrid and mean!
All the flowers stand around,
knowing you'll never let them down.

Every dawn you're covered in dew,
while the morning mist swirls around you.
Red, yellow, pink and white,
you come in so many colours bright.

Your strong sturdy stem,
holds you upright.
Your pretty green leaves
create food using light.

You are the flower of romance
the soul and spirit of a dance.
The perfect gift for Valentine's Day,
a lovely rose bouquet!

Nikhita Vasani (11)
Teesside Preparatory & High School, Stockton-on-Tees

Fit For Life

My name is Amelia, I like to keep fit.
I like to run and I like to skip.
I try to keep healthy, lay off the sweets
But have a little sugar to make you fit.

I'm not skinny, I'm not fat,
I eat loads of fruit and lay off the tat.

I'm fit for life, that's what I am
And stay off the sweets and sugary jam.

Amelia Bruce (10)
Teesside Preparatory & High School, Stockton-on-Tees

Skiing

The mountain
has whooshing air
flying through
your hair.

Rushing down
the mountain
soaring through
the snow.

Skiing through
the forest
branches sticking out,
don't go any faster
then you zoom out.

Feet getting tired
start to moan
and groan,
hot chocolate
waiting for you
when you
get home.

Joanna Lister (8)
Teesside Preparatory & High School, Stockton-on-Tees

Trees

As tall as a skyscraper
As green as the grass
As shady as a palm leaf
As big as a bulldozer
As brown as mud
As sticky as a slimy snail.

Adya Trivedi (8)
Teesside Preparatory & High School, Stockton-on-Tees

A Spring Walk

Wellingtons on
lead in hand
through the field
dandelions yellow
grass green.

Corn sways in the wind
he springs, jumps, runs
nose in the air
scent, stops, points
a pheasant clucks.

Into the valley
stream trickles
birds twitter
he returns
tongue hanging, panting loud
running to the water.

Up to the wood
ash, pine, oak trees we pass
to the rapeseed fields
oceans of yellow
leading to the farm
lambs black and white.

Whistle, whistle, whistle
Luca! Luca! Come here boy
finally home!

Anna Lucia Orlandi (10)
Teesside Preparatory & High School, Stockton-on-Tees

Castles

There are lots of different castles,
So this is about them all.
Some castles are haunted and scary castles
Towered up really tall.

Fairy tale castles are really grand,
They have crystal walls and shiny halls.
Candyfloss floors and sweet rock doors
And on the roof there's candy balls.

Royal castles are really smart,
They have glamorous walls and golden doors.
If there's any dust the maid will clean it up
But if not the king will have wars.

Haunted castles are really spooky,
If you step on a step it will be really creaky.
When you walk it will be so noisy,
You will think your new shoes are all leaky!

Larissa Sofia Nath (9)
Teesside Preparatory & High School, Stockton-on-Tees

The River

Twisting, turning, the murky blue stream
Winding down the tropical forest
Trees towering, swaying in the breeze
The soft and calming trickle echoes through the forest

As it winds it way forward with awesome power
It ripples and runs like strokes of lightning
It halts and is intimidated
By the sheer drop that tires so many fearsome brooks before it.

Alicia Preston (11)
Teesside Preparatory & High School, Stockton-on-Tees

Regret

Power, power
I wanted to see
Lay deeply scolded
Embedded in me.

As I worked harder and harder,
I got higher and higher
Until madness took over
The top of the spire.

Though I was rich
No money to borrow
I would weep and wail,
Cry in sorrow.

All this sorrow,
A piercing stab
Power now took over,
The love I once had.

Holly Brownlee (11)
Teesside Preparatory & High School, Stockton-on-Tees

Sea Orchestra

The clarinet is like seaweed popping,
The bass drum is the shark ready for attack,
The violin is like the seagull squawking,
Flying around, around the sea.

The flute is like the dolphins jumping,
The cello is the whales' song,
The piccolo is like the sea horses hopping,
Swimming around, around the sea.

The double bass is like the waves crashing,
The trumpet is the fish scuttling away from danger,
The oboe is like the ripple of the waves,
Calmly around, around the sea.

Hannah Hunter (11)
Teesside Preparatory & High School, Stockton-on-Tees

What Is Wrong With Me?

Oh what is wrong with me?
I thought I could pass my GCSE.
But I failed in every test,
At least I tried my best.
I suppose an F is not too bad.
What I fear is telling my dad.

Oh what is wrong with me?
In the maths test I'm last out of 63.
I couldn't get the algebra,
The sums were way too hard,
Let alone the long division,
I think it should be barred.

No there's nothing wrong with me,
At last I can really see,
I'm a superstar at dancing
Of that I'm really sure.
You should have seen me at the dance contest
Spinning around the dance floor.

So it all goes to show,
And I'm sure you already know,
If in one thing you fail to shine,
In another you will do fine.

Lydia Neave (11)
Teesside Preparatory & High School, Stockton-on-Tees

Fireworks

Fireworks are beautiful,
Fireworks are bright,
Fireworks are the best on a dark night.
Crackle, pop, they all go,
Bang, boom, whee,
They all sizzle with glee.

Francesca Doyle (7)
Teesside Preparatory & High School, Stockton-on-Tees

Jobs That I Would Have

The first job I would have
would be a police lady, yes siree.
Helping people around the world,
yes that's me.

The next job I would have
would be an actor,
standing on the stage
with all the people laughing at me
and cheering me on.

Then after that I would be a singer,
standing on the stage,
everyone listening to me.
To sing is just a great feeling to have.

If that didn't turn out
I would be a cook instead.
Letting people try my food,
makes me feel like a respected cook.

But right now I am a bit too young
to do all that.
All I would like to do
is just sit down and read a book.

Vanessa Okey (11)
Teesside Preparatory & High School, Stockton-on-Tees

What Is Orange?

Orange is a juicy fruit
A sun with a warm and welcome feel
Orange is a beaming glow
Or when I cuddle up in bed.

Orange is sitting by the fire
On a cold winter's night
Sunsets and happy smiles
Orange is the best colour I think.

Hope Barker (8)
Teesside Preparatory & High School, Stockton-on-Tees

A Misty Morning

The mist went
Whirling,
Twirling,
Curling,
Around the tall, imposing houses,
Swallowing them up to time indefinite,
Daring them to try to challenge it away.
All on a cold, crisp Saturday morning.

People were lured into it,
Encircled,
Enveloped,
Entwined,
Like a baby in swaddling.
Gradually fading into the thick white cloak,
That concealed everything in its path.
All on a cold, crisp Saturday morning.

As the mist faded they were gradually freed from
Whirling,
Twirling,
Curling,
Around the old Victorian lamp posts.
All on a cold, crisp Saturday morning.

Naomi Duncan (11)
Teesside Preparatory & High School, Stockton-on-Tees

Me

Today I feel very fine
Never been better
Happy, friendly,
Loveable as well.
Cuddles and snuggles
And more each day.
Happy and cheery we play
Till the sun sinks away.

Hollie Blake (7)
Teesside Preparatory & High School, Stockton-on-Tees

Phantom Manor

Sliding windows,
creaking doors,
winding stairs,
dusty floors.
Mysterious articles glide around,
but not a trace of life is found,
deathly transparent figures roam,
in that sorry abandoned home.
The ghost of a woman who died years ago,
'death by husband' apparently so.
A phantom dog rabid and infected,
a small deformed kitten cruelly rejected.
Sliding windows,
creaking doors,
winding stairs,
dusty floors.
Mysterious articles glide around,
in Phantom Manor, silent and sound.

Anna Harrison (10)
Teesside Preparatory & High School, Stockton-on-Tees

What Is Gold?

Gold is treasure
In the Queen's palace.
Gold is rich.
What if the world
Was made of gold?
What if everyone
Was the colour gold?
Golden glasses, golden pears
Gold is everywhere.
I love gold.

Nusha Fazeli (7)
Teesside Preparatory & High School, Stockton-on-Tees

Happiness

Happiness is sky blue
It lies sweetly around you,
It runs through the air,
Blows through your hair
And runs around giving happiness,
To people like you.

Happiness smells like newly cut grass,
From the countryside,
It feels like a warm, cheerful feeling
That is growing inside you day by day.

Happiness sounds like people
Laughing and joking
But most of all having lots of fun
With their friends and family.

Happiness tastes like
A refreshing drink on a hot day.
Happiness is like a kind, warm, gentle,
Caring feeling that everyone should have.

Happiness is the ability to share,
To show others that we really care.
Happiness is to forgive.
Happiness is friends and family
Uniting on special occasions.

Happiness brings friends to one another.
Happiness is a cloudless sky,
That greets us every morning.
Happiness is baby lambs
Playing in their fields each day.
Happy is what we should all be.

Sally Mohammed (11)
Teesside Preparatory & High School, Stockton-on-Tees

The Eagle

Eagle, eagle, swirling softly in the sky
What a beautiful magnificent sight
How will we find your nest?
Are you going to have a rest?

Where will you go, over land or sea?
Will you fly right up in the sky
Or hunt on the floor for your prey?
In the night you peacefully lay.

Your feathers shine brightly in the bright blue sky
To frame your magnificent features
Or to hunt silently for your prey
Are you going to eat small creatures?

Eagle, eagle, swirling softly in the sky
Where will you go now?
Will you go on holiday
Or will you stay here for your prey?

Eagle, eagle, silently, softly falling to the ground
What will you dream of? Nobody knows.
Where will you go? Nobody knows.
Now after this day have a rest in your nest.

Megan Roach (11)
Teesside Preparatory & High School, Stockton-on-Tees

What Is Yellow?

Yellow is a dandelion
that shines in the sun.
Yellow is some cheese
that fits in a bun.

Yellow is the sun
that shines in the sky.
Yellow is a bird
that's nice when it flies.

Kitty Fox (8)
Teesside Preparatory & High School, Stockton-on-Tees

The Highwayman

Suddenly, appearing out of the gloom,
a fearful sight, a sense of doom,
washes o'er the naive passer-by,
upon hearing that fateful, haunted cry.

For riding, melting out of the haze
appear men, do evil in thousands of ways.
Poor innocent traveller knows his hour has come,
for creatures of terror are the highwaymen.

Suddenly, silently, a shot rings out,
a cry of pain, a stifled shout,
then falls, lying on the floor,
the wretched traveller is no more.

Swiftly, noiselessly, they ride away,
enough money to live for one more day,
but soon 'nother guiltless man shall die,
with no one but criminals to hear his cries.

Katherine Wren (11)
Teesside Preparatory & High School, Stockton-on-Tees

Teenagers

Sulky glances, disco dances
Smiles and laughs a little rare
Fashion shocking, boys come knocking
Flirty glances, say I dare.

Father ponders, Mother wonders
Where's the nice young girl we knew?
Stamping, moaning, always phoning
Friends who seem the same way too.

Fast lane living, take not giving,
We just ask, keep her from harm
Steps may falter, she will alter
Our love for her will ride the storm.

Hayley Anderson (11)
Teesside Preparatory & High School, Stockton-on-Tees

Everyone But Me

I dread the time when the school bell rings,
Everyone rushes to the playground but me.
I sit on the bench reading my book,
While other children gossip and have fun.

I dread the time when the school bell rings,
Everyone rushes to the playground but me.
I wander to my spot, on the wall,
Where children mock me all through break.

I dread the time when the school bell rings,
Everyone rushes to the playground but me.
They shove me, drag me and swing me around,
Kick me, thump me and yell names.

I feel so glad when the school bell rings,
Everyone rushes through the playground behind me.
I'm out of the gate as quick as a flash,
Sprinting home, feeling free once more.

Natalie Garner (11)
Teesside Preparatory & High School, Stockton-on-Tees

Good Luck

I'm writing this poem for memories in the future,
I'm boosted up with confidence from my friends and my teacher,
I'm working so hard for some extra pride,
And all the good luck is on my side.
Write down some words with extra care,
I'll enter the competition, shall I, will I dare?
My friends and family are wishing me good luck,
Let's hope it will get published in the book,
In my mind all the thought and creation,
Oh how I'm using my imagination.

Robyn Yawson (11)
Teesside Preparatory & High School, Stockton-on-Tees

My Brother Rob

My brother Rob
Is in the RAF
That stands for Royal Air Force
If you could not guess.

He's been playing guitar for a year or two
And yet he's on grade 6
And when he puts up campfires
He uses several sticks.

Of course he is annoying
He does make lots of noise
And every day he pinches
At least one of my toys.

He's also in the CCF
That's Combined Cadet Force
He marches always up and down
Behind soldiers on a horse.

He's at the age of 17
He really wants a job
But at the end of the day
I am glad that he's my brother Rob.

Emma Kiczma-Walsh (10)
Teesside Preparatory & High School, Stockton-on-Tees

Flowers

F lowers are beautiful like the first snow of the season.
L oyal and faithful they are, just like you.
O pen and free with no burdens to carry.
W ild and untamed until they wither away.
E very day they seem to amaze us more and more.
R oyal like royalty, they are Mother Nature's favourite.
S pecial and important and they will be forever.

Chloe Thuta (10)
Teesside Preparatory & High School, Stockton-on-Tees

Little Sisters

Little sisters are built to annoy,
'Let me play, give me that toy!'
Their endless campaign of 'I want to play'
Goes on and on, night and day.
When I want some peace and quiet,
They begin their terrible riot!
Their threatening of 'I'll tell Mum',
Goes on and on, as if for fun!
Their yells of anger, yowling, screeching,
As they begin their deafening preaching!

They're like a toy wound up too tight,
As they carry on into the night.
Then you give in and let them play
They say 'Maybe another day!'
They then begin another wail,
That makes you wish they were in jail.
Then Mum's voice cries up the stair,
'Jenny be nice, play fair!'
Then I wish I was rid of that blister,
My moaning, wailing little sister!

Jenny Lister (10)
Teesside Preparatory & High School, Stockton-on-Tees

My Emotions

My fear is insects, bugs or ants,
My excitement lifts me up and makes me want to dance,
My calmness is a hurricane howling and blowing,
My bravery is when I stand up to someone on my own,
My shyness usually shows up on the phone,
My happiness is family and friends,
My sadness is when time spent with them ends.

Lucy Dougall (11)
Teesside Preparatory & High School, Stockton-on-Tees

Willow

Willow here, there, very popular is the willow,
always blowing like a gale, always going,
flowing to and fro in the wind I blow.

Next to the river I stand, my little legs
holding me up nice and strong.
My little arms swaying here and there,
between the river moonlight they stare.

Twisting here, twisting there,
through the trees they have to go,
further and further in the trees they flow.

In thine night, never stopping like a ghost
only in the twinkling twilight of the moon's light.

Always on the go, I move with the flow,
never stopping, never still.

When darkness falls I play dead,
when morning strikes I feel reborn.

Abigail Metcalfe (10)
Teesside Preparatory & High School, Stockton-on-Tees

Me

Hannah is my name
Blue-eyed, blonde-haired girl
Funny, caring, helpful
Like a multicoloured fish in the sea
Like a book that has not been read
Full of imagination and happiness
Like a firework waiting to explode
Hannah is my name
Reminds me to always be myself.

Hannah Bell (11)
Teesside Preparatory & High School, Stockton-on-Tees

Magic

A spellbinding secret that really isn't real,
Made by witches and wizards,
Who have magical pets like snakes,
Parrots, lizards and even cats,
They live in secret caves and castles,
Moving everything around by one special finger,
Some are good and some are evil,
They are usually riding on broomsticks
Or even vacuum cleaners,
I never thought I'd see a witch or warlock,
Until one tragic night, my dad was reading,
My mum was sewing, all very happy,
Then we heard a cackle and a scream
And a black figure falling,
We ran to see but all was quiet,
So if you ever see a figure falling from the sky,
Beware, *beware!*

Hannah McGloin (10)
Teesside Preparatory & High School, Stockton-on-Tees

Autumn Leaf

An autumn leaf falling from the sky.

An autumn leaf
Falling, falling, blowing, blowing
Autumn leaves flow in the breeze, falling from the high trees
It falls like a feather and is as golden as the sun.
As green as the grass
It's greener than a grass snake

An autumn leaf lands on the ground
As quiet as a mouse
As soft as a pillow
The leaves land in a pile
Colours of gold, yellow, green and pink
How beautiful!

Cecilia Neave (7)
Teesside Preparatory & High School, Stockton-on-Tees

I Remember

I remember when the sun used to set
Behind a light green hill,
As I gazed the sky turned black
Through my window sill.

I remember when I was young
I sat upon a tree,
After hours my mum would shout,
'Come have your tea,' to me.

I remember when I got married
In a church one day,
He placed a ring upon my finger
Then bowed down to say.

I remember when my husband died
In a car crash one night,
The police came round and told me
It gave me such a fright.

But now I'm 93
I wear a big red fleece,
I'm in a hospital right now
And soon I'll rest in peace.

Beth Taylor (9)
Teesside Preparatory & High School, Stockton-on-Tees

Bluebirds

Bluebirds, bluebirds
under my bed
bluebirds, bluebirds
purple and red.

Bluebirds, bluebirds
flying up in the sky
bluebirds, bluebirds
eating bread and pie.

Bluebirds, bluebirds
nasty and mean
bluebirds, bluebirds
eating ice cream.

Bluebirds, bluebirds
on my knee
bluebirds, bluebirds
on a tall tree.

Bluebirds, bluebirds
on my head
bluebirds, bluebirds
goodbye, you are dead!

Flutter, flutter
flutter, flutter!

Jasveen Kaur Jagpal (10)
Teesside Preparatory & High School, Stockton-on-Tees

Animal Habits

Snakes slither,
Mice dither.
Kangaroos jump,
Camels take the hump.
Fish swim,
Monkeys make a din.
Tigers growl,
Lions prowl.
Kittens fight,
Dogs bite.
Deer leap,
Koalas sleep.
Bees hum,
Elephants like a bun.
Squirrels climb,
Tortoises take their time.
Parrots talk,
Birds squawk.
Giraffes eat,
Goats bleat.
Snails are slow,
Jellyfish go with the flow.
Cheetahs race,
Foxes chase.
Rabbits nibble,
Worms wiggle.
Butterflies flutter,
Whales splutter.
Jaguars kill,
Sloths stay still.

Ellen Parker (10)
Teesside Preparatory & High School, Stockton-on-Tees

The Elves' Castle

Once in time again,
In a little tree,
The sun will ever shine,
And the elves will have their tea!

A castle is this humble home,
For elves, not you or me,
There, while the queen sits and sings,
The elves will have their tea!

The walls, made from crystal,
The venue, by the sea,
Peep through the window,
The elves are having their tea!

Everyone's asleep, time for bed,
Dream away, to that little tree,
But wait, everyone's asleep,
The elves have had their tea!

Becky Donaldson (9)
Teesside Preparatory & High School, Stockton-on-Tees

The Man From Japan

There once was a man from Japan
Who carried a large frying pan
He hit his friend's head
And got sent to bed
And next day he carried a fan.

James Barwick (9)
Valley Road Community Primary School, Sunderland

A Young Girl From Spain

There was a young girl from Spain
Who didn't like being in the rain
It flattened her hair
Made her look like a bear
And caused her feelings much pain.

Sophie Howell (9)
Valley Road Community Primary School, Sunderland

Happy

Happy is pink like a sunset
It tastes of sweet strawberries with cream.
It smells like strawberry milkshake.
It looks like a funfair.
It sounds like High School Musical.
It feels like being with friends.

Karen Redpath (9)
Valley Road Community Primary School, Sunderland

The Man From Japan

There once was a man from Japan
Who held a big frying pan
He whacked his friend's head
And got sent to bed
When he saw him again his friend ran.

Ryan Barwick (9)
Valley Road Community Primary School, Sunderland

Happiness

Happiness is pink like candyfloss
It tastes like strawberry milkshake
It smells like the calm sea
It looks like a love heart
It feels like being at home.

Lewis Herron (9)
Valley Road Community Primary School, Sunderland

Happy

Happy is multicoloured like rainbow sweets
It tastes like a chewy lolly
It smells like mixed perfume
It looks like a multicoloured world with blue people
It sounds like Shakira singing
It feels wonderful.

Stembie Muchegwa (9)
Valley Road Community Primary School, Sunderland

Love

Love is pink
It tastes like strawberry chocolate
It smells sweet
It looks like love hearts
It sounds like flying love hearts
It feels exciting.

Bradley Potts (9)
Valley Road Community Primary School, Sunderland

Ten Naughty Children

Ten naughty children standing in a line
one got run over and then there were nine.
Nine naughty children running through a gate
one got hit by a football and then there were eight.
Eight naughty children on their way to Devon
one went to Heaven and then there were seven.
Seven naughty children got up to many tricks
one bit his hand off and then there were six.
Six naughty children looking at a hive
one went to space and then there were five.
Five naughty children thought they saw some straw
one ate some and then there were four.
Four naughty children tried to climb a tree
one fell off and then there were three.
Three naughty children didn't know what to do
one hit himself with a shovel and then there were two.
Two naughty children tried to eat a bun
one choked and then there was one.
One naughty child having lots of fun
he shot himself and then there were none.

Joe Gleave (8)
Whitley CP School, Warrington

Five Naughty Children

Five naughty children waiting by the door
One got locked inside a cupboard and then there were four.
Four naughty children playing with a key
One ran into the cloakroom then there were three.
Three naughty children visiting the zoo
One was eaten by a lion then there were two.
Two naughty children sitting in the sun
One got rather sunburnt and then there was one.
One naughty child going for a run
Tripped over his shoelace and then there were none.

Rebecca Tart (8)
Whitley CP School, Warrington

Ten Naughty Children

Ten naughty children standing in a line
one said a rude word then there were nine.

Nine naughty children running through a gate
one thought he would vault it then there were eight.

Eight naughty children on their way to Devon
one slipped off a cliff then there were seven.

Seven naughty children got up to many tricks
one played one on the headmaster and then there were six.

Six naughty children looking at a hive
one stuck his head in then there were five.

Five naughty children thought they saw some straw
one was run over by a tractor then there were four.

Four naughty children tried to climb a tree
one jumped from a height then there were three.

Three naughty children didn't know what to do
one forgot he had detention then there were two.

Two naughty children tried to eat a bun
one was really rock hard then there was one.

One naughty child having lots of fun
suddenly the teacher came then there were none.

Matthew Clayton (9)
Whitley CP School, Warrington

The Brilliant Footballer Patrick

There was a great footballer called Patrick
He scored a brilliant hat-trick
The crowd gave a cheer
And so did Mrs Lear
That wonderful footballer Patrick.

Daniel Newsham (9)
Whitley CP School, Warrington

Say No

I am a bully
Big and strong
I can knock off your head
And do no wrong.

Don't be afraid
Come and join me now
If you don't come along
We'll have a row.

I have no friends
I am all alone
I need to be nice
In school and at home.

I am an ex bully
Big and strong
We are all friends
This is where I belong!

That is the end of my bullying life.

By an ex bully!

Tara Moore (8)
Whitley CP School, Warrington

Whether The Wind

Whether the wind be fine,
Whether the wind be not,
Whether the wind be cold,
Whether the wind be hot,
Whether the weather,
Whatever the weather,
Whether you like it or not.

Sophie Norddahl-Payne (8)
Whitley CP School, Warrington

How Did The Children Leave The Classroom

Robin Race ran out of the classroom.
Salma Ballet danced out of the classroom.
Tom Ball dribbled out of the classroom.
Helen Skip skipped out of the classroom.
Tony Snail slithered out of the classroom.
Jasmin Joy went joyously out of the classroom.
Ryan River flowed out of the classroom.
Chloe Tap tapped out of the classroom.
Ken Bounce bounced out of the classroom.
Mary Fish swerved out of the classroom.

Becky Connell (9)
Whitley CP School, Warrington

Talking To The Class

Mrs Loud screeched to her class
Mr Grumble moaned to his class
Ms Quiet whispered to her class
Mr Bell tinkled to his class
Miss Bee buzzed to her class
Mr Wolf howled to his class
Mrs Frog croaked to her class
Mr Bird twittered to his class
Mrs Bangham boomed to her class
And Miss Melody sang to the whole school.

Charlotte Barker (8)
Whitley CP School, Warrington

Seven Things About Him

He lived far away down in Kent
On my long train journey off I went

He was a relative of mine
But I didn't see him all of the time

He was not very well so he moved to a home
So he wouldn't have to live alone

When he moved to the home, we bought him a blue teddy
I've written about this teddy, in school a lot already

He died on the 4th June, it was a sad day
I miss him so much in every way

He was a funny man
He was the father of my nan

I love him so much
'Him' is my great grandad Jim
(I have still got the blue teddy to remind me of him).

Ellis Judge (9)
Whitley CP School, Warrington

Who Am I?

Mouse-chaser
Mess-maker
Softy-snoozer
Jumping-loser
Climbing-rider
Annoying-hider
Dirty-eater
Snacking-feature.

Who am I?
A: a cat.

Kate Straughan (10)
Whitley CP School, Warrington

Young Writers Information

We hope you have enjoyed reading this book - and that you will continue to enjoy it in the coming years.

If you like reading and writing poetry drop us a line, or give us a call, and we'll send you a free information pack.

Alternatively if you would like to order further copies of this book or any of our other titles, then please give us a call or log onto our website at www.youngwriters.co.uk

Young Writers Information
Remus House
Coltsfoot Drive
Peterborough
PE2 9JX

(01733) 890066